The
New Taste of
Chocolate

# The
# New Taste of
# Chocolate

## A Cultural & Natural History
## of Cacao with Recipes

*Maricel E. Presilla*

TEN SPEED PRESS
Berkeley ■ Toronto

Ten Speed Press
Box 7123
Berkeley, California 94707
www.tenspeed.com

Distributed in Australia by Simon & Schuster Australia, in Canada by Ten Speed Press Canada, in New Zealand by Southern Publishers Group, in South Africa by Real Books, and in the United Kingdom and Europe by Airlift Book Company.

Cover and book design by Toni Tajima
Copyediting by Andrea Chesman
Principal photography by Roberto Mata and
    Maricel E. Presilla.
Food and prop photography by Frankie Frankeny on the
    cover, and pages ii, 20, 60, 67, 81 (top), 118, 121, 125, 128,
    137, 141, 143, 147, 161, and 175.
Recipe testing and food styling for Frankie Frankeny
    photography by Wesley Martin.
Additional recipe testing by Sarah Wallace and
    Marc Severino.
Maps and prints from Maricel E. Presillas's collection on
    pages v, 9, 13, 25 (top), 27, 28, 29, 35, 40, 43, 56, 64 (left),
    75, 87, 96, 97, 107 (top), 109, 111 (bottom), and 129.

Library of Congress Cataloging-in-Publication Data
Presilla, Maricel E.
    The new taste of chocolate: a cultural & natural history
of cacao with recipes / by Maricel Presilla.
        p. cm.
    Includes bibliographical references and index.
    ISBN 1-58008-143-6
    1. Cookery (Chocolate) 2. Chocolate I. Title.
    TX767.C5 P74 2000
641.6'374—dc21
    00-062035

Printed in China
First printing, 2001

3 4 5 6 7 8 9 10 — 08 07 06 05

**The following material is reprinted with permission:**

Pages v (portrait), 1 (background), and 5 (top) by Ismael Espinosa Ferrer. Author's collection.

Pages viii, ix, and 180–198: Rosary bead detail from the *Códice de Yanhuitlán,* Lámina XXVIII (Rosario de Cuentas de Oro). Courtesy of the Instituto Nacional de Antropología e Historia, Mexico.

Page 5 (bottom): Courtesy of The New York Public Library.

Page 8: Courtesy of The North Carolina Museum of Art, Raleigh, North Carolina.

Page 12: From the *Codex Mendoza,* MS. Arch. Selden. A.I., folio 47r. Courtesy of the Bodleian Library, Oxford.

Page 14: From the *Códice de Yanhuitlán.* Courtesy of the Instituto Nacional de Antropología e Historia, Mexico.

Page 17: Courtesy of Giraudon, Paris.

Page 18 (bottom): Courtesy of the López Memorial Museum Collection, Manila.

Page 19: From the *Códice Tudela.* Courtesy of the Museo de América, Madrid.

Page 20: Courtesy of Fondo Cultural Cafetero, Colombia.

Page 21: Courtesy of The New York Public Library.

Page 25 (bottom): Photo by Kike Arnal.

Page 30: Courtesy of Chocovic S.A., Spain.

Page 31: Quote reprinted with permission from Alfred A. Knopf, Inc.

Page 32: Map by Susan Ziegler.

Page 36: Photo courtesy of The New York Public Library

Page 39: Photo courtesy of Frances Bekele, Cacao Research Unit (CRU), Trinidad.

Page 50: Document courtesy of Silvino Reyes and Ana Karina Flores Luxat.

Page 58: Photo by Kike Arnal.

Page 72: Courtesy of The New York Public Library.

Page 80 (top): Courtesy of Steven Wallace, Omanhene Cocoa Bean Company.

Page 83 (backdrop): Courtesy of Biblioteca Real Jardín Botánico, Madrid, CSIC.

Page 94: Courtesy of Gladys Ramos Carranza.

Page 95 (bottom): Photo by Kike Arnal.

Photo 105: Courtesy of Steven Wallace.

Page 109 (bottom): Photo by Kike Arnal.

Page 111: Photo courtesy of Silvio Crespo.

Page 112: Map by Susan Ziegler.

Page 119 (backdrop): Courtesy of Galerie Rauhut, Munich.

Page 165: Photo by Teri Sandison, courtesy of Guittard Chocolate.

Page 169: Photo courtesy of Gonzalo Galavís.

Page 174: Photos by José Buil Belenguer. Courtesy of the Archivo General del Estado de Veracruz. Collección Juan Manuel Buil Güemes.

Page 176: From the *Códice Azoyú,* folio 21. Courtesy of the Instituto Nacional de Antropología e Historia.

To the memory of my grandmother Pascuala Ferrer Matos,
who was born with cacao, and for my family the Ferrer clan of
the Jauco River and Baracoa, who still live with cacao.

With gratitude to my aunt Ana Luisa Espinosa Ferrer and
my father Ismael Espinosa Ferrer for remembering it all so well.

# Contents

*Acknowledgments*    viii

*Growing Up with Cacao*    1

*A Natural and Cultural History of Chocolate*    9

*From Cacao to Chocolate*    43

*Identifying Cacao*    83

*Tasting Chocolate*    119

*Recipes*    129

*Glossary*    180
*Sources*    184
*Select Bibliography*    190
*Index*    193

# Acknowledgments

In 1999, I went back to Cuba to revisit my first memories of cacao. I found my paternal family, the large Ferrer clan, still clinging to their cacao and coffee farms in the same remote place where my Spanish great-grandfather and his Cuban wife had settled after their wedding in 1889. Manolo, Mireya, Manolito, Eve, Nelson, Jaime, Blas, Faustino, and Evelio Ferrer, their spouses and their many children, opened their doors and hearts without reservation. My heartfelt gratitude to all of them, and the ones who are no more, for the gift of cacao.

Special thanks to my friends and associates Silvino Reyes and his wife, Ana Karina Flores Luxat, the owners of Hacienda La Concepción, for drawing me into cacao farming and the cacao bean trade. Time and again, Arsenio Borthomierth, the manager of La Concepción, has cut through thick undergrowth with his machete to open a path for me and my camera. For his expertise and kindness I'll be forever grateful. My thanks to the workers of La Concepción: Eduarda Martínez, Virgilia Córdoba, José Cartagena, Remigio Rodríguez, Winston Salazar, Miguel Martínez, Marcelino Hernández, Giovanni Heredia, Alexander Fariñas, Ignacia Martínez, Nelly Martínez, Rafael Martínez, Gertrudis Mantel, Mireya Ojeda, Francisco "Tabaco" Rodríguez, Gabriel Rodríguez, and Luisa Heredia. I would also like to express my gratitude to Wilfred Merle of the Proyecto Paria, Juan Sardi, and the cacao workers of APROCAO for making my visits to the cacao plantations of the Paria Peninsula such a pleasure. My thanks to Francisco (Pancho) Bolívar, a member of Chuao's cooperative for his assistance. In Chuao, I found the best guides I could hope for: children Oliver Bolívar, Cristobal Manuel Infante, and Hernán Enríquez Liendo Bolívar.

I owe a great debt to renowned scientists Humberto Reyes and his wife, Lilian Capriles de Reyes, for teaching me about the intricacies of cacao agriculture. I am very grateful to Gladys Ramos Carranza, the head agronomist of the Campo Experimental San Juan de Lagunillas, for introducing me to Guasare cacao. Antonio Azócar, the station's field manager, assisted me in many details. I am indebted to Nancy Arroyo for her support during my work at the Estación Experimental Chama in the flatlands of Lake Maracaibo. My thanks to Kai Rosenberg for inviting me to visit La Sabaneta, his colonial cacao plantation in Choroní. I am specially grateful to agronomist Beatriz Escobar for her friendship and warm hospitality at the Finca San Joaquín. In Trinidad, cacao grower Philippe Agostini allowed me to roam over San Juan Estate. My thanks to Pooran Ramdoolar, the farm's overseer, for guiding me through the maze of the Cheesman Field. My gratitude to Dr. David Butler, head of the Cocoa Research Unit in Trinidad, for allowing me to watch the work of cacao scientists at close range. With Dr. Thayil Sreenivasan, an expert on cacao pathology, I took a look at cacao's many scourges. Researcher Darin Sukha guided me through the International Cocoa Genebank. Morphology expert Frances Bekele was my cacao muse; not only did she help me identify the pods I collected in Trinidad, but she answered every query with patience and enthusiasm. My appreciation to Julie Reneau, research scientist at Nestlé R&D Centre at York, UK, for her insights on chocolate tasting, and CIRAD researchers Olivier Sounigo, molecular biologist, and Jean-Marc Thévenin, plant pathologist, for answering my many questions.

My thanks to Jorge Redmond, president of Chocolates El Rey, for giving me the opportunity to assist in the birth of a world-class Latin American chocolate. On every visit to El Rey's factory, Alfredo Zozaya and Alfred Meyer were my guides, showing me every nook and cranny. César Guevara, was a most valuable font of information on cacao agriculture in Venezuela. Rand Turner was generous in providing products for recipe tasting. Thanks to Roger Thürkauf, formerly of Suchard and Maestrani, for the important lessons in chocolate manufacturing. My gratitude to my cousin Jorge Ferrer, the chemical engineer of the chocolate factory of Baracoa, for introducing me to another side of the Cuban cacao industry.

Silvio Crespo, former technical director of Wilbur Chocolates, gave me a glimpse of the inner workings of the North American chocolate industry and shared valuable insights on the art of blending. With Robert Steinberg and John Scharffenberger I had the fortune of witnessing the birth pangs of an exciting new North American chocolate. Many thanks to Terri Richardson and his assistant Peter Dea for going out of their way to help me in this project. Thalia Hohenthal of Guittard Chocolates taught me a memorable lesson on the science of cacao butter. My gratitude to Gary Guittard, president of Guittard Chocolates, for his ongoing support. Special thanks to cacao broker Roland Sánchez for taking time from his busy schedule to keep me abreast of the vagaries of the international cacao trade. Thanks to those who provided products and information: Mario Snellenberg, Export Director of Chocovic S.A.; Jean-Jacques Berjot of Barry-Callebaut, Canada; Bernard Duclos of Valrhona Chocolates; Steven Wallace of Omanhene Cocoa Bean Company; and François Pralus.

Many thanks to Jim Graham for sharing his vast knowledge of tempering; Tish Hall and Timothy Moriarty of *Chocolatier* magazine for introducing me to many wonderful pastry chefs; Rachel Akselrod for useful contacts; Susana Trilling for her kind assistance; chef Philippe Chin for his generosity; chef Helena Ibarra for helping me cook with fresh cacao; Marc Bauer and Vicky Wells, my pastry teachers at FCI, for all things chocolate; Mirza Salazar and Paloma Ramos, my assistants, for their devotion; and Raquel Torres for inviting me to apprentice at her restaurant in Xalapa, where drinking hot chocolate is still a ritual. In 1992, I had the fortune of meeting food historian Sophie D. Coe at an Oldways conference in Spain; her spirit lives on in her indispensable book *The True History of Chocolate,* which was completed by her husband, anthropologist Michael D. Coe. Harold McGee taught me more about the science of cacao fermentation than any textbook. My sincere appreciation to chocolate artist Elaine González, who took me under her wing and provided leads to the world of chocolate confectionery. My profound gratitude to my friend and fellow food historian Anne Mendelson for her invaluable work on my manuscript. Anne read my work with a sharp eye, correcting my mistakes and offering learned advice.

Special thanks to the dynamic Ten Speed Press team. First, my heartfelt gratitude to my editor Lorena Jones, who edited with sensitivity and intelligence. Thanks to her unwavering support *The New Taste of Chocolate* is a beautiful book that makes me happy. My deep appreciation to assistant editor Brie Mazurek for her dedication and for taking care of so many details. Thanks to senior editor Aaron Wehner for adding fun to the equation, and to publicist Lisa Regul for caring. I am most grateful to Phil Wood and publisher Kirsty Melville for taking a chance on a book about cacao. I was lucky to work with talented book designer Toni Tajima, who translated my vision into a thoughtful and elegant design. I am also indebted to art director Nancy Austin for giving me the means and the freedom to do justice to the beauty of cacao.

In Venezuela, I teamed up with photographer Roberto Mata, whose photos make this book truly special. Thanks also to his assistant Daniel Mazaira. Grateful acknowledgment to Venezuelan photographer Kike Arnal and Gonzalo Galavís for their important contributions. My appreciation to Daniel Fábrega, who assisted me during my work in Central America. My gratitude to my father Ismael Espinosa for his line drawings. Thanks also to Susan Ziegler for her hand-painted maps. Many thanks are due to the people and institutions who have granted reprint permissions and supplied visual materials, specially Rose Mary and Rainer Rauhut, Joseph González, and Ralph E. Magnus.

Special thanks to all the enlightened chefs and chocolate experts who have contributed their recipes and insights to this book. My gratitude to my friends and business partners at Zafra, Clara Chaumont and Leonardo de la Sierra, for holding the fort while I was putting the last touches on this book. I owe much to my friends Marc Aronson and Marina Budhos, who offered advice and shared the joy of chocolate at my table. My thanks also to Nelly and Saul Galavís for being the most generous hosts I could ever hope to find in Barquisimeto. I owe an enormous debt of gratitude to food journalist Miro Popiç and his wife, Yolanda, and their children, Maikel and Veronika, for becoming my family in Caracas and for letting me turn their house into a cacao warehouse and busy center of operations. This is a better book because of Miro. Many thanks to Maria Guarnaschelli for her cheerful, steadfast support.

Finally, my eternal gratitude to my husband Alejandro Presilla, who has not only tolerated the cacao flies that arrived with my first bag of cacao beans, but who has encouraged me to take a plane at a moment's notice to do my work right. Alex has helped me photograph and pick cacao pods in many steamy plantations, lending his considerable technical skills—and equipment—every time I needed to set up a makeshift photo studio in the clearing of a forest, a hotel room, or our dining room. This book also belongs to him.

# Growing Up with Cacao

For many people, tasting just a small piece of chocolate can trigger a flood of memories, whether it's of their first Hershey bar or that special cake baked for a birthday or a graduation. It's not quite like that for me. I am fortunate to be a Latin American with long memories drawn from something closer to chocolate's origin. I first got to know it as a fruit.

## A Strange and Wonderful Fruit

When my father told me about big, strange-looking fruits that sprouted right out of the tree bark and were filled with the beans that are the source of all chocolate, I formed a mental picture of thick-skinned papayas full of fragrant Hershey chocolate kisses. Then one day he brought home about a dozen cacao pods from his mother's family farm at the eastern end of Cuba, about eighty miles from our home in Santiago.

They were large oval fruits of many shapes and hues: some rounded and smooth, others longer with bumpy skins and long-ridged grooves, colored in splendid shades of orange, russet, yellow, and green. I was entranced until my father cut open the first pod. Instead of chocolate-colored beans to eat like candy, I found a strange mass of lumpy, tan-colored seeds enclosed in a sticky, glistening ivory pulp that did not even smell like chocolate.

My father scooped out the inside of the pod and gave me some of the pulp to suck on. It had a refreshing sweet-tart flavor and a won-

ABOVE: In the upper Jauco River region of eastern Cuba, cacao farmers carry cacao pods, fruits, and coffee beans in *catauros*—sturdy baskets made with *yaguas*, the hard sheathing bracts of royal palm leaves. My cousin Carlos Espinosa takes a newly made *catauro* to our family's hilly cacao grove.

1

derful aromatic quality that today reminds me of lychees. If you ever taste fresh cacao fruit, you will understand what attracted people to it long before the discovery of chocolate.

I would have eaten the lot happily, but my father, who is an artist, had other plans. He had brought them back to paint. For days I had to endure the sight of those luscious pods arranged in a basket until they shriveled up. I still remember how much I longed to eat that cacao and to go to the place it came from.

It was several years later that I visited the farm, high in the forested mountains of the upper Jauco River, not far from the southeastern tip of the island. My great-grandparents, Desideria Matos and Francisco Ferrer, who originally came from Alicante, Spain, settled in this isolated and godforsaken area at the end of the nineteenth century. As the Cubans put it, they quickly became *aplatanados*—that is, they went native like plantain trees. In their new home at Cañas they began a typical anything-and-everything, mixed-growth farm, living off the land by growing and processing the things they needed, right down to their own home-roasted coffee beans and home-crushed sugarcane juice, which they used for sweetening when they couldn't get commercial sugar. Cacao was sold for cash.

The cacao farm was small and lush, with the deceptively chaotic look characteristic of the tropics, where many kinds of plants are crammed together in a planned give-and-take. My father's elderly uncles and their children tended the cacao growth and harvested the fruit with sharp blades fixed on long poles. The pods were collected in a rustic rectangular bas-ket called a *catauro,* made from palm fibers. The men cut open the pods with machetes, removed the mass of beans embedded in the white pulp, and squeezed out as much pulp as they could by hand. Then the beans were spread out on a cedar tray fitted with wheels to dry in the sun. At night, or when it rained, the tray was wheeled into a thatched shed. After a few days, the pale tan beans changed to a reddish brown color and were ready to be bagged for sale.

## Taking Chocolate into Their Own Hands

Meanwhile, at the ranch house, another batch of beans was being transformed into chocolate. The aunts and cousins roasted the cacao out-doors—like coffee beans—over a wood fire in a large blackened kettle. Then, they ground the roasted beans into a sticky, fragrant paste in a hand-cranked corn grinder and mixed it with sugar and flour. They rolled the paste between the palms of their hands to make balls the size of duck eggs. These were set out to dry. When needed, they grated chocolate off the hard surface, dissolved the gratings in water or milk, and heated it to make a thick hot drink.

How powerful and knowledgeable these women seemed to me, taking chocolate into their own hands! Later I would always remember that I belonged to those who live with cacao and know it personally, as a tree, a fruit, an ordinary household preparation.

Today thousands of such people still live in the cacao-growing regions of Latin America, where the plant originated and chocolate

LEFT: Cacao balls (center) made with *criollo* cacao and flavored with aromatic spices, for sale at Mérida's central market in the Venezuelan Andes

BELOW: Street signs in Papantla, a vanilla-producing town in northeastern Veracruz state, Mexico, announce the arrival of freshly harvested cacao beans from Tabasco and Chiapas and homemade chocolate.

reached its early heights of development. For them, this is a fruit as rooted in the land as potatoes. They are not mystified or intimidated by even the finest commercial chocolates. They, too, have taken a batch of beans and made chocolate.

The chocolate that so fascinated me was meant to be consumed as a drink—the way the Aztecs and their subjects knew cacao, the way it is mainly used throughout Latin America today. Wherever cacao grows in the New World, someone is harvesting the beans on a small farm or buying them by the kilo at a market to make the same kind of cacao balls for drinking chocolate that my peasant family made at Cañas.

That early memory links me with Latin American chocolate at its plainest and most democratic, economically extended with thickeners. Yet the Ferrer clan's rough-and-ready drink also lingers in my memory when I taste

the sophisticated hot chocolate of small artisanal producers in other Latin American regions, from Oaxaca in Mexico to the Paria Peninsula in Venezuela. The complexly layered interaction of fine, skillfully treated cacao with half a dozen Old and New World spices transports me to Spanish colonial drawing rooms with elegantly gowned ladies sitting on low,

Luis Ferrer, my father's uncle, built this cacao drying house atop a steep hill overlooking the Jauco River. This drying system—with minor structural variations—is found all over the Caribbean from Martinique to Trinidad—the beans are spread on a wooden platform that can be wheeled under an A-frame shed at night or during rain.

Drying Cocoa.

Traditional drying sheds on the island of Trinidad

cushioned stools to sip frothy, spiced hot chocolate from hand-painted gourds or thin porcelain cups.

## Bridging the Information Gap: Getting to Know Chocolate from Bean to Bar

In 1994, when I was asked to be a marketing consultant for a respected Latin American chocolate producer, I began to taste, travel, read, correspond, and experiment with an eagerness far beyond what was required of me. Once again I found myself drawn to aspects of the subject that didn't seem to be a part of the general European and American chocolate experience. I saw that even at high levels of connoisseurship, there was an information gap—a lack of communication between those who consume and cook with chocolate and those who produce it.

Probably the watershed events in my realization were the Venezuelan tours on which I led groups of American and European chefs and journalists through some of the finest cacao plantations in the world. As they walked through the farms, I saw their vision of chocolate expanding to take in the living tree and everything that goes into its nurture.

The true appreciation of chocolate quality begins with a link between the different spheres of effort. To know chocolate, you must know that the candy in the box or the chef's creation on the plate begins with the bean, with the complex genetic profile of different cacao strains. Think how impossible it would be to make fine coffee with the coarse, acrid beans of *Coffea robusta*. You must know also that the flavor of the finished product further depends on people carrying out careful, rigorous harvesting and fermentation practices.

Today, most informed cooks and diners appreciate the many intertwined factors that add up to quality in products like tea, coffee, cheese, and wine. Somehow chocolate has not received the same scrutiny. My Venezuelan trips showed me that chocolate lovers are eager to bridge the gap when offered the opportunity. In fact, I detect something cooking, a quiet revolution in the perception and enjoyment of chocolate. I am starting to see a deeper understanding of cacao's essential nature among a new breed of chocolate manufacturers in developed nations, spearheaded by new outreach efforts on the part of enlightened growers, manufacturers, and researchers in some cacao-producing countries.

Now, perhaps, you will understand why I have written this book with a modest but important mission. I want as many chocolate lovers as possible to marvel at the pre-Columbian beginning and Spanish colonial flowering of chocolate. I want you to understand the many factors—genetic, chemical, environmental—that determine the quality of chocolate at all stages, from the fertilized flower to the foil-wrapped bar. I want to take you inside the thinking of the scientists who identify and develop important cacao strains. And I want you to see the human face of cacao farming. The life of a plantation worker in the Third World should mean as much to the chocolate lover as that of the chef who transforms a bar of chocolate into a work of art.

More than two hundred years ago, Carolus Linnaeus, the great Swedish founder of modern botany, bestowed on the cacao tree the scientific name *Theobroma cacao,* or "food-of-the-gods cacao." Truly, for many people, chocolate is as close to celestial as any food can be. But I hope that through this book you will find an equal fascination in the story of its roots in the earth, and learn to see it as a food of the people.

Workers take baskets of freshly harvested cacao beans to be weighed at the farmhouse of Hacienda la Concepción in Barlovento, Venezuela.

# A Natural and Cultural History of Chocolate

"Where there is cacao, there is life," a Venezuelan plantation worker once said to me, referring to both his own livelihood and to the nurturing relationship between cacao and the land. No tree has more to teach us than cacao, when we take the trouble to see it in its own environmental and biological context.

In nearly every part of the world where cacao trees are raised today, they are surrounded by other useful plants that shade them at different points in their life cycle. The true cacao—*Theobroma cacao,* Linnaeus's "food of the gods"—is perfectly adapted to the demands of the humid New World tropics, which lie roughly within the latitudes of 20 degrees north and 20 degrees south of the equator. At least twenty remarkably similar wild Latin American cousins in the *Theobroma* genus live in the shadowed forest understories today. One of them, *Theobroma bicolor* or

*patashte,* is a food crop in Mexico and Central America. Another has enough culinary merit to have become an important domesticated crop of its own: *Theobroma grandiflora,* the prized *cupuaçu* fruit of the Brazilian Amazon. These plants share the habit of putting forth flowers from cushionlike patches on the trunk (a condition called "cauliflory") and displaying all stages of flower and fruit growth year-round.

The origin of cacao is a subject mired in controversy, but most modern scientists argue that cacao first grew in South America. Recent DNA analysis pin-

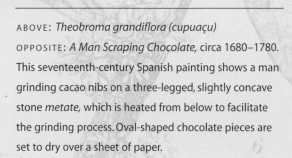

ABOVE: *Theobroma grandiflora (cupuaçu)*
OPPOSITE: *A Man Scraping Chocolate,* circa 1680–1780. This seventeenth-century Spanish painting shows a man grinding cacao nibs on a three-legged, slightly concave stone *metate,* which is heated from below to facilitate the grinding process. Oval-shaped chocolate pieces are set to dry over a sheet of paper.

*Theobroma speciosum*. This cacao relative bears stunning clusters of dark red flowers.

## Cacao Enters the Kitchen

Historians have not established when, how, or why cacao began to be carried north. By the end of the first millennium B.C., the variety of cacao native to northwestern South America seems to have been already on the move. The plant's first migration in a long series of world travels was into the tropical forests covering parts of modern Mexico and some of its Central American neighbors. It was here that someone first looked past the delicious gooey white interior of the multicolored cacao fruits to the almond-sized seeds enclosed in each pod.

Some historians speak of this development as a miraculous leap, pointing to the fact that a cacao seed (officially "bean") in its natural form is an unpromising and usually bitter object. But it's not that simple. The culinary investigation of the beans seems logical and inevitable, given the systematic way in which the pre-Columbian cuisines of Mesoamerica approached most of their standard foods. What they did with the astringent but oil-rich beans was spread them to dry in the sun, roast them on clay *comales* (griddles), and then grind them on stone slabs—all everyday techniques used with such common foods as chiles, pumpkin seeds, and corn. The miraculous part is not that they tried the same procedures on cacao but that these procedures chemically transformed it into something almost unrecognizable—chocolate. The sweet pulp softened and melted by itself or was rinsed away with the fibrous material ("placenta") holding it together. The interior of the beans fermented to some degree in the sun; other compounds were formed during roasting.

points two areas that gave rise to two slightly different genotypes, or genetic makeups. One was the Amazon River basin. The other lies in modern Venezuela, south of the udder-shaped Lake Maracaibo and in the foothills of the Venezuelan and Colombian Andes.

In the beginning, the different members of the cacao complex found their local niches—and incidentally, spread different parts of an original genetic dowry according to nature's own choreography. Then something triggered an unknown chain of events that would transform sturdy wild plants occupying well-based environmental nooks into a particularly valuable crop transplanted into precarious new circumstances.

Grinding the roasted seeds released their oils along with other volatile substances produced in the earlier treatments, creating an irresistibly fragrant paste that could be shaped into little cakes or balls and dried for future use.

This is not a dim historical footnote en route to real chocolate, meaning modern chocolate industrially processed for candies and cakes. The first Mesoamerican discoverers of chocolate achieved the great feat of domesticating the plant and growing it in an ecologically sound way. They arrived at a sophisticated knowledge of chocolate's culinary possibilities, combining it with a wide array of other ingredients—vanilla, herbs, flower petals, chiles, maguey sap, honey, mamey sapote pits, and achiote—to create flavors and effects that make our uses for chocolate pale in comparison. This traditional concept of chocolate has never wholly died out in Mexico and other parts of Latin America.

## Born in the New World

What people began the Mesoamerican chocolate story? Perhaps it was the little-known Gulf Coast Olmecs, or perhaps it was the Maya, who mastered the drying-roasting technique and set about grinding the treated cacao together with chiles, other spices, and sometimes coloring agents like the reddish achiote seed. Mixtures like this still exist. They were, and are, used in a variety of hot and cold chocolate beverages, though "beverages" is really a misnomer. The cooking of Mexico and neighboring regions has always been rich in drinkable foods that fit no European category. Chocolate became prominent in two branches of the family: flavorful gruels and porridges (from quite thin to nearly solid) based on ground corn and highly prized creations with frothed toppings, like the Veracruzan *popo* or the Oaxacan *tejate*.

Before the Spanish came, frothed drinks were often used as sacred offerings (a use that

**THE ULTIMATE WHIPPED CREAM**

In Oaxacan markets, you are likely to find several grades of fossil-like cacao beans. When the beans are whole, their deep black exterior encloses a crumbly, ivory-white calcified interior. These are the beans of *Theobroma bicolor,* which have white cotyledons (the crumpled-up tissues that would unfold into leaves if the seeds were planted). They have been buried in lime for several days to turn them this way. Oaxacans use them to make a firm foam to top a thick corn porridge called *atole.* Think of this foamy topping as the ultimate whipped cream.

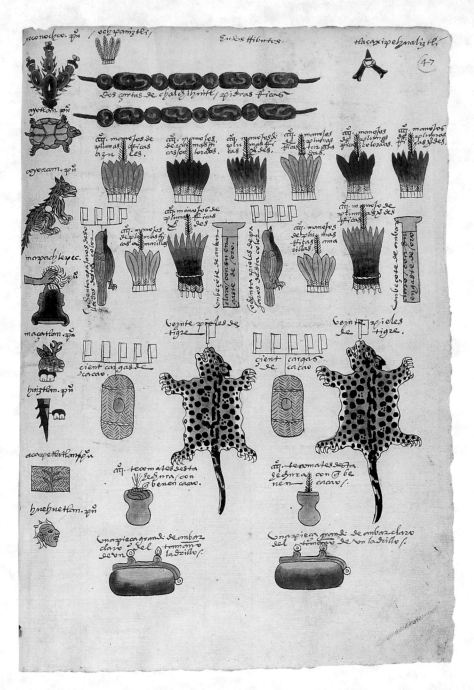

This folio from the sixteenth-century *Códice Mendoza* records the tributes paid to the Aztec rulers twice a year by the subject cacao-growing region of Xoconochco (Soconosco). Besides jaguar skins, cotinga feathers, and the prized green stone chalchihuitl, Xoconochco provided Tenochtitlán with 200 loads of freshly harvested cacao and 800 gourds to drink chocolate. According to the sixteenth-century Spanish chronicler Fray Toribio de Benavente (Motolinía), a load of cacao was equivalent to 24,000 beans.

persisted into modern times in scattered spots). Even today they retain some ceremonial aura. In Oaxaca the froth on the top of chocolate drinks represents a gift of personal vigor or essential force from the one presenting to the one receiving the drink. The idea of a chocolate-enriched corn gruel also survives today in the universally popular Mexican *champurrado* and its many Latin American cousins, like the *chorote* of Tabasco and the Venezuelan Andes, and the Ecuadorian *chocolate con máchica,* chocolate thickened with toasted barley flour.

Many people today connect chocolate with the Aztecs, but they did not discover chocolate on their own, for the cacao tree would not grow anywhere near their strongholds in the high central valleys of Mexico. When the Aztecs conquered large parts of Mexico starting in the late fourteenth century, they eagerly adopted and extended the uses of chocolate that they found being prepared in the southern parts of their empire. By the 1520s, when the Spaniards began poking around the Mexican Caribbean and Gulf coasts, cacao was not only one of the most extraordinarily valuable items traded on the mainland, it was also routinely carried hundreds of miles to satisfy appetites in Tenochtitlán, the great Aztec capital. Like other goods, such as cotton, feathers, or the precious dye called "cochineal," cacao also formed part of the tributes paid to the Aztec court by subject provinces. In the post-conquest illustrated manuscript called the *Códice Mendoza,* we find records of cacao tributes being sent in baskets, jars, or bales to the capital from five southern provinces. The cacao beans grown in Xoconochco (later Soconosco)

in the present-day state of Chiapas were particularly valued, and the *Códice Mendoza* records an annual tribute of two hundred loads.

By then cacao had taken on the status of legal money. This is how Columbus was introduced to it on his one and only encounter with cacao. In 1502, on his fourth New World voyage, Columbus, who was accompanied by his teenaged son Ferdinand, intercepted a party of Indians in a massive canoe off the coast of

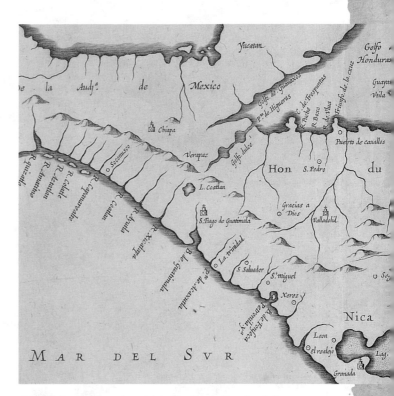

*Descripcion del Destricto del Audiencia de Guatimala* by Antonio de Herrera, 1601/1622. The "Audiencia" (the Spanish colonial political division immediately below the viceroyalty) of Guatemala encompassed Guatemala, Honduras, Nicaragua, and Costa Rica. The map shows the important cacao-producing areas of Tabasco, Chiapas, and Soconosco.

today's Honduras. Later, Ferdinand wrote of the surprising fuss the people made over some nuts that they carried with them, stooping to rescue any that dropped "as if an eye had fallen from their heads." Since neither group spoke the other's language, the reason would remain a mystery until Cortés's army marched into Mexico seventeen years later.

The *Códice Yanhuitlán* (1532–1556) documents the consolidation of Spanish political and economic power in Santo Domingo Yanhuitlán and other Mixtec towns in Oaxaca, Mexico. Yanhuitlán was an important middle point in the cacao trade between the cold highlands of Mexico and the warm cacao-producing region of Soconosco during the early colonial period. Here we see the Dominican friar Domingo de Santa María, known for his evangelical work among the Mixtecs and his knowledge of agriculture.

## As Good as Gold

*The cacao dealer customarily has a large quantity of it and has plantations of cacao, and brings it out to sell. The good dealer in this commodity, the beans that he sells are all fat, solid, and select. And he sells each thing separately, in one place the ones that are fat and solid, and in one place the ones that are small and hollowed, or broken, and in one place their broken-up pieces. And each kind by itself: Those from Tochtepec, those from Anáhuac, those from Guatemala, those from Guatulco [Huatulco], those from Xoloteco, whether they are whitish, or ashy, or red.*

BERNARDINO DE SAHAGÚN (1499–1590),
*HISTORIA GENERAL DE LAS COSAS DE
LA NUEVA ESPAÑA*

Nearly all of what we know about cacao and chocolate in Mexico before the Spanish invasion comes from what the conquistadors wrote down afterwards. They paid great attention to anything smacking of wealth. Struck by the use of cacao beans as specific units of money (commodities ranging from turkeys to sex had their known price in cacao) and by the notable social prestige attached to chocolate as a drink, they were predisposed to be interested. Cortés and his companions observed the Emperor Moctezuma drinking frothed chocolate with a degree of ceremony, clearly marking it as an exalted food. The conquerors saw that cacao ranked with gold and gems in records of solemn offerings to the dead. They gathered that its use was restricted to the noble and military classes. We do not know how clear their grasp of Aztec society was, but there is no doubt that when their hosts presented them with cacao, and invited them to partake of prepared chocolate, the gesture was meant as a great honor.

The first wave of Spanish missionaries brought a keen observer: the Franciscan friar Bernardino de Sahagún, who compiled a monumental account of the Aztecs in their own language and translated it into Spanish. From his descriptions, we can see that the Mexican peoples were informed connoisseurs of cacao and chocolate, and also that the Spaniards accurately absorbed much of that knowledge.

What always impresses me most in the early accounts is the Indians' awareness of cacao and its qualities. Let's go back for a moment to the first true cacao—the one that originally grew in South America, along with many wild descendants of the first cacao ancestor or ancestors. In reality, true cacao trees (*Theobroma cacao*) were never uniform copies of a standard model. There must have been many built-in variations in each of the two principal geno-types. But the one we are concerned with in its adoptive Mexican home—the strain that might have originated around the northern Andean foothills and in the flatlands below Lake Maracaibo, or perhaps (as some scientists will still argue) arose independently in Mesoamer-ica—had certain strongly expressed qualities

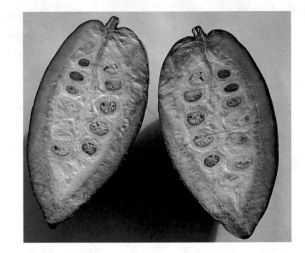

ABOVE: This transverse section of an unripe *porcelana* pod from western Venezuela shows the characteristic pure white and light pink cotyledons of a true *criollo* pod with red skin.

LEFT: From svelte cacao trees with their outlandish fruits to a box of seductive bonbons, there is an improbable distance that does not look any shorter when you first cut into the fruit. Your first impression is of slimy lumps embedded in a nameless whitish substance that recalls squashed insect larvae or other unpleasant sights. The whiteness is disconcerting because when you think of chocolate, dark brown is the key color you recall.

that help determine the character of any chocolate made from it.

The cacao that grew in Mexico is distinguished by large, plump beans. When cut open, the raw beans reveal very pale, pure white to light pink cotyledons. The taste is somewhat bitter but not unpleasantly astringent. When the beans are fermented and roasted, faintly nutty or delicately herbal overtones in the raw cacao deepen into a more pronounced accent of nuts, and you start to detect other flavor notes from fruity or flowery to spicy.

Wherever this first strain of cacao was domesticated in Mesoamerica, it took on a slightly different local character or *goût de terroir*. Sahagún's account makes it clear that shoppers in the Aztec marketplace were knowledgeable and choosy about the beans shipped north to them from cacao-growing territory. They paid for quality and were always on the lookout for adulteration.

The best dealers arranged their stores of cacao by place of origin, as we might distinguish between Blue Point and Cotuit oysters. When the Spanish colonists began their own chocolate experiments within about a generation after Cortés, they continued to observe these crucial distinctions and to judge chocolate on the basis of nuances in the different original cacaos it was made from. Later they would attach names like *cacao dulce* (sweet cacao) or *cacao blanco* (white cacao) to the whole complex of superior cacaos that they had found being grown in Mesoamerica and later in Venezuela. But the name that would endure was *criollo*, or "born in the New World."

## The Drink of Aristocrats:
### Old World Transformations

Spain adopted the habit of drinking chocolate early in the seventeenth century. Within fifty or sixty years, the custom had spread to France, Italy, England, and most parts of Europe. Meanwhile, the taste for drinking chocolate had already taken hold in the Spanish colonial cities of Mexico like San Cristóbal de las Casas in Chiapas—where women were known to drink gourdfuls during mass. In colonial Caracas, chocolate drinking was all the rage, and the wives of the cacao barons drank it at the lavish mid-afternoon soirees called *agasajos,* as was the fashion in Spain.

This Hispanicized chocolate was loosely inspired by what Cortés had found the Aztecs drinking, and it emphasized the idea of a complex, heavily spiced mixture. The Spaniards even embraced some of the porridge dishes the Indians had created, such as chocolate thickened with *pinole*—a blend of ground, toasted corn and spices such as vanilla and achiote (annatto). They turned one former option into a requirement: adding a sweetener. It was the Spanish who first married chocolate and sugar, which they and the other European colonial powers were busy planting with African slave

Detail from *The Cup of Chocolate* by Jean-Baptiste Charpentier le Vieux (1728–1806). A French aristocrat drinks chocolate from a delicate porcelain cup.

ABOVE: *Mole* is a thick, baroque sauce that is made with dozens of ingredients, including chocolate. These are the ingredients for a traditional *mole* from Xalapa, Veracruz. All are processed in sequence, each at its own time.

BELOW: The *metate* became as much at home in Spain, France (where it was called "the Spanish stone"), and the Philippines as in Mexico. A Chinese servant in Manila grinds *criollo* beans on a Mexican *metate*.

labor throughout the Caribbean. Pre-Hispanic Mexico had no sugar; cooks used honey or the sap from the heart of the maguey plant when they wanted to sweeten chocolate. Starting around the late seventeenth century, another development may have occurred simultaneously in Europe and colonial Mexico: the use of chocolate as a spice or flavoring in savory dishes, from the Sicilian *caponata* to the Catalan *estofados* (braised dishes) and several of the hybridized Spanish-Indian *moles* of Mexico. But the lion's share of attention to chocolate during the seventeenth and eighteenth centuries went to its incarnations as a beverage.

One thing that didn't change—at first, anyhow—was the association of drinking chocolate with high social standing. It arrived in Europe with the aura of an exotic luxury for the cognoscenti. Both the making and the drinking involved special pains and paraphernalia. Someone had to roast the beans over a fire (carefully judging the degree of doneness so that they developed full flavor without scorching), lightly crush them to facilitate removing the thin shell or thick skin covering each bean, and, using a mortar and pestle or a stone slab modeled on the Mexican *metate*, grind them to a grainy paste with other ingredients. Before the age of mechanization, *metates* had an amazing intercontinental and multiethnic career wherever chocolate went. The rest of the mixture matched the exotic-luxury image. It might feature several spices (often cinnamon and anise, with or without nutmeg and some form of chile or other pepper), essences (rosewater or orange-blossom water), ground nuts (typically almonds, hazelnuts, pine nuts, and/or pista-

THE NEW TASTE OF CHOCOLATE

*Códice Tudela*, sixteenth century. A Mexican woman prepares a chocolate drink with a frothy head by pouring the liquid back and forth between two vessels.

chios), such New World ingredients as achiote and vanilla, Old World rarities (ambergris, musk), and, of course, sugar, which was still a food for the rich. Any dry ingredients not ground with the chocolate had to be pounded to a powder and sifted.

The rich cacao oils would tend to rise to the top when the mixture was combined with hot water or (a European innovation) milk. The new breed of chocolate aficionados generally skimmed off some of the fat, and partly offset the effect of the rest by beating up a froth on the drink. Bypassing the many foam-

ing agents that were and still are made from native Mexican plants, they frothed the chocolate by the technique (also Mexican) of repeatedly pouring it back and forth between two vessels, or whipping it with a clever device called a chocolate mill *(molinillo)* in which wooden rings rattled briskly around a stick twirled between the palms. At first, Spaniards drank chocolate in gourds—some lavishly decorated. Soon exquisite porcelain cups were being manufactured for the serving of chocolate, and a special pot had been devised with a built-in mill.

LEFT: *Afternoon Chocolate in Colombia,* watercolor, by Joseph Brown (1802–1874). The cult of hot chocolate flourished during the colonial period in the cool highlands of Colombia, in cities such as Bogotá. In Brown's vignette of the traditional afternoon repast, an Indian woman serves hot chocolate to a European visitor.

RIGHT: *Molinillos*

THE NEW TASTE OF CHOCOLATE

## The Genetic Plot Thickens:
## The Coming of Forastero

The pleasures of the chocolate pot ultimately came from African slave labor. The need for slaves came from a New World labor crunch that developed after millions of Indians died—apparently of diseases brought by the conquerors—just as Old World demand for the new taste sensation of hot chocolate began to expand beyond everyone's wildest dreams.

With this new labor supply, cacao production expanded during the late seventeenth and eighteenth centuries. But after a time, discerning judges began to find that some of the cacao coming from the American plantations was surprisingly inferior. This is where the genetic plot thickens. It is difficult to document exactly what happened at just what date, but the end result is clear: At some point in the eighteenth century (possibly earlier), a new source of genes was introduced into the world's commercial cacao stocks. The consequence was a widespread and lasting change in the quality of chocolate, and the repercussions are still being felt today.

To understand what happened, we must return to the two genotypes of true cacao that originated in South America. For the sake of convenience, I will call these genotypes (or races of cacao) by the names that they acquired much later in the history of the cacao business: *criollo,* the northern South American strain that came to Mesoamerica, or arose independently there, and was introduced to the Spanish, and *forastero,* the strain that apparently began in the Amazon basin. In historical sources, the use of these terms is far from consistent, but today they are standard.

For several generations after the Spanish and Portuguese conquests, Amazonian cacao remained unknown to the chocolate trade. But its day was coming. By the mid-seventeenth century, both of these Iberian powers had discovered luxuriant stands of something they recognized as cacao growing wild or semiwild on the South American mainland, especially in Ecuador and along the course of the Amazon. Here the native people knew it as a fruit, but it had never made the great leap to chocolate.

Anyone acquainted with *criollo* cacao would have found the other cacao strains

West African workers sun-dry *forastero* cacao beans on raised movable wooden trays.

strangely foreign, which is actually the meaning of the word *forastero*. The fruits were thick-skinned—some were smooth and rounded, rather than pointed and warty. The beans within the pods had a flattened rather than plump shape, and in the interior of the beans, the cotyledons were a medium or deep purple instead of white or rosy white. The differences in taste were just as obvious. The raw beans had a harsher bitterness than the familiar *criollo*

type. When fermented (which took longer) and roasted, they retained an acrid, sour quality and a different aroma. The chocolate made from them was strong-flavored but flat, with nothing of the mellowness and complexity of the *criollo* beans. Yet *forastero* cacao had some overwhelming advantages. The trees reliably produced many pods with a large bean count and appeared very hardy, which was becoming much more important to growers.

LEFT: A transverse section of an Upper Amazon *forastero* pod shows the thickness of the husk (cortex or pericarp) and the spatial configuration of the beans within the pod with five rows of flat beans attached to a central placenta.

RIGHT: At least ten percent of the cells making up the tissue of the seed's two cotyledons contain anthocyanins (among other polyphenols). These chemicals give *forastero* cotyledons a deep purple color. The cotyledons of all *forasteros* feature varying shades of purple, except the white-cotyledon Brazilian *catongo* (*Theobroma leiocarpa),* which is a mutant form of *forastero* that contains no anthocyanins.

OPPOSITE: A smooth-skinned *forastero calabacillo* pod

## Blast! Trinitarios Are Born

The rise of *forastero* was linked to the problems the growers were beginning to encounter with their treasured *criollo* cacao. During the chocolate boom, the Spanish had found it impossible to revive Mexican production to pre-plague levels. Indeed, Mexico became a net *importer* of Venezuelan cacao in the seventeenth century, and Spaniards had put their eggs in other baskets. Early on, the Spanish took Central American cacao—probably from Nicaragua—to the valleys of Venezuela's central coast and to the Hispanic Caribbean islands. *Criollo* types probably passed from Venezuela to the neighboring island of Trinidad (a subject mired with controversy) at an uncertain time.

All seemed well at first. The Venezuelan producers made fortunes in the lucrative cacao trade, now supplying Mexico as well as Europe. But by about 1725 they found themselves facing disaster. A series of epidemics swept over the cacao groves; probably the first recorded one was a mysterious event that wiped out the plantations of neighboring Trinidad in 1727. An English account calls it a "blast," which at that time commonly meant "blight." The Valencian Jesuit Joseph Gumilla, an eyewitness of the catastrophe, saw the barely formed cacao pods falling when they were only the size of an almond and announced that it was a divine judgment on people who didn't pay their tithes to the church. After a few years, the growers tried to reestablish their plantations with stock brought from the Orinoco basin in eastern Venezuela. The mainland trees rapidly crossed with the remains of the old *criollo* growth on Trinidad. The growers found themselves with a hybrid cacao—hardier than *criollo* and better tasting than *forastero*—which they named *trinitario,* after the island.

LEFT: Two *trinitario* pods

OPPOSITE, TOP: *Venezuela cum parte Australi Novae Andalusiae* by Henricus Hondius, 1642. This dramatic Venezuela map extends from Rio de la Hacha to Trinidad and the mouth of the Orinoco and includes the Lesser Antilles up to Dominica.

OPPOSITE, BELOW: The Orinoco River

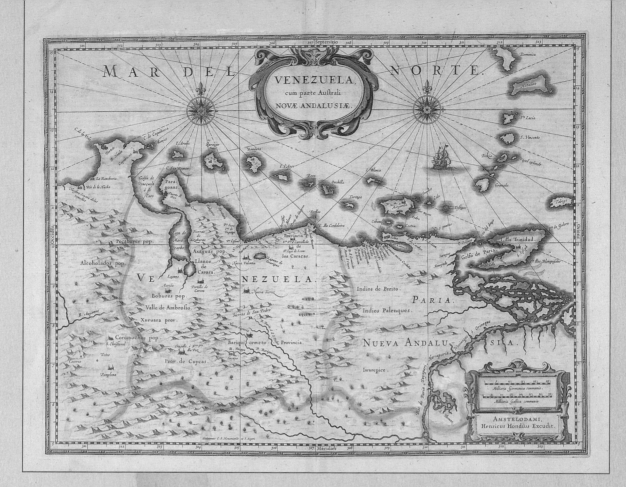

## FROM VENEZUELA TO TRINIDAD

Many retrospective guesses have been made about the nature of the original *trinitario* population of the island. We surmise that the cacao brought to Trinidad years after the blast must have been *forastero,* or—if spontaneous crossing between the two genotypes had already been going on—they must have had a lot of Lower Amazon *forastero* in their makeup. E. E. Cheesman, the botanist working at Trinidad's Imperial College of Tropical Agriculture, who wrote a seminal work on cacao in 1944, speculates that the Trinidadian planters found new *forastero* stock in the area around Ciudad Bolívar on the lower course of the Orinoco. The Venezuelan scientist Humberto Reyes suggests that the two races of cacao might have hybridized first in the Orinoco delta. The *forasteros* of this area, Reyes adds, exhibit the wide range of morphological variations (see page 84) found today in *trinitarios*. He infers that *criollo* could have been easily carried by man from the foothills of the Andes through the river network that led to the Orinoco and then to the delta area. In the eighteenth century, trade and most contacts between Trinidad and Venezuela took place through the Orinoco River.

## A Promiscuous Trio

Many classifications of cacao list an official trio of *forastero, criollo,* and *trinitario*—A, B, and A x B. However, everything is much more complex than that. The original *forasteros* and *criollos* underwent not one but hundreds or thousands of crossings and back crossings since *forastero* was discovered by the growers. They may have previously hybridized here and there in the wild to form different subvariants. It is not clear that *trinitario* itself ever was just one single strain resulting from one encounter of the two original parents. The name now applies to many different cacao clones—that is, groups of plant specimens propagated by grafting slips onto pieces of rootstock in order to preserve the genetic identity of a single parent. But it is certainly clear that a plethora of *forastero* and *criollo* offspring came into being in many cacao-growing regions as soon as people started planting the two genotypes together, and that only DNA analysis can ever unscramble the resulting mixes of genes. The other fact beyond dispute is that the more *forastero* genes got into the world cacao supply, the less accustomed consumers became to the taste of chocolate made with pure *criollo* cacao.

From the eighteenth century on, the share of *forastero* grew by leaps and bounds until today it accounts for more than 90 percent of the cacao used by the world's chocolate manufacturers.

A page from *El Orinoco Ilustrado* by Joseph Gumilla, 1741. Nothing escaped the keen intellect of the Valencian Jesuit Joseph Gumilla, the great historian of the Orinoco River. He recorded the life of Indian communities, flora (including cacao) and fauna, and even the trials and tribulations of the farmers of neighboring Trinidad. Here, he notes that only the cacao trees of N. Rabelo, a pious farmer from the Canary Islands, were spared from the "blast"—a sure sign "that God had rewarded his punctuality" in paying the tithe to the church.

## From Nuanced Luxury to Daily Snack

European and colonial Latin American connoisseurs knew a lot about the origin of their chocolate. They did not generally use the names *criollo* or *forastero*, but they identified most cacao by the name of the area in which it was grown. Soconosco and Caracas ("Caraque" to the French, "Carack" to the English) beans were considered the *crème de la crème*. The Soconosco came from an area of Chiapas that used to send cacao tribute to Aztec emperors; the Caracas came from the Venezuelan regions that sent cacao to the port of La Guaira, near the city of Caracas. Equally valued was Maracaibo cacao, brought from the foothills of the Venezuelan Andes and the southern environs of Lake Maracaibo and shipped from Maracaibo port. Cacao dealers and chocolate makers might even vie for beans from a single prestigious plantation, such as the fabled Venezuelan estate of Chuao. These highly valued cacaos were among the purest *criollos* surviving after *forasteros* and *trinitarios* invaded the world market, and they commanded high prices. The quality of the beans could be tasted in the finished chocolate—until a new technological age dawned.

For many years cacao beans were roasted and ground into a thick, grainy paste (cacao

A copper etching by Benard of an artisanal chocolate shop in France, from the *Encyclopédie*, 1715. The workers in this small shop are shown carrying out the same basic operations performed by the women in pre-Columbian and colonial times. The dried beans are (1) roasted, (2) winnowed, or shelled, (3) ground with a mortar and pestle, and (4) ground again with flavoring ingredients into a very fine paste on a heated *metate*-like grinding stone.

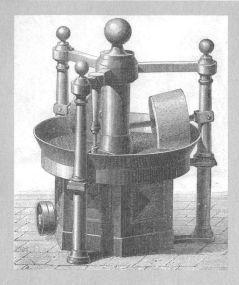

The mélangeur (shown here in a wood engraving by Spamer, from *Orbis Pictus*, 1874) is one of the most versatile and long-lasting inventions of the industrial revolution of chocolate manufacturing. in the nineteenth century. In *Cocoa: All about It,* Richard Cadbury, under the pseudonym "Historicus," described it:

> The pure Cocoa is, in the first place, incorporated with white sugar in what is called a "Melangeur." This mixing machine consists of a round granite revolving slab, forming a pan, the sides being of steel. Into this receptacle the Cocoa and sugar are poured, and two sets of heavy, stationary, granite rollers bruise the thick mass, which is reduced to the consistency of dough. A double knife, the action of which is similar to that of a screw pro-peller, continually revolves just above the rotary stone slab, and distributes the Chocolate as it passes.
>
> —RICHARD CADBURY, 1896

mass or liquor), by methods differing very little from the pre-Columbian *metate,* except that during the eighteenth century small factories succeeded in carrying out the work on a some-what larger scale. Then, in 1828, Conrad Van Houten of the Netherlands developed a way of mechanically extracting most of the fat from the cacao liquor, resulting in "cacao butter," which could be used for anything from soap to suppositories, and the partly defatted "cocoa," a compacted mass of solids that could be sold as it was ("rock cocoa") or ground to a powder. This cocoa furnished a quick drink far eas-ier to make than the traditional hot chocolate. In addition, the cacao liquor and cacao butter could be recombined by confectioners in any attractive proportion to make something even more lucrative: eating chocolate.

In Europe, cocoa technology began the transformation of chocolate from an exquis-itely nuanced luxury to an inexpensive daily snack. The voluptuous and costly spices of the old-style hot chocolate were abandoned in the industrial product. Cocoa mixed with sugar soon became a drink of the masses. It con-tained no extraneous flavors, yet paradoxically the basic chocolate flavor mattered less. What the cocoa drinker was tasting was not the essential, whole cacao itself, but an industrially broken-down and reconstituted part of it. Often the original cacao was further denatured by Van Houten's other contribution, an alkali treatment that made the cocoa mix more smoothly while darkening the color and offset-

A turn-of-the-century Catalan mélangeur is still in use at the choco-late factory La Locomotora in Xalapa, Veracruz.

ting the natural acidity of poorly fermented or poor-quality beans.

The next step forward was a smoother chocolate. The product made by the first European chocolate fans and early commercial chocolatiers had a distinct graininess, which was not a fault but an intrinsic quality of the food itself. This was eliminated by a process introduced in 1879 by the Swiss Rodolphe Lindt. He added another stage to the process of grinding the roasted cacao with sugar. The Lindt innovation, known as "conching," was to agitate the ground mass—either unmodified, or more often, adjusted with additional cacao butter—in a sloshing-and-kneading apparatus called a "conche," which was inspired by the Mesoamerican *metate*. The mass was processed for hours on end (usually more than twenty-four, sometimes more than seventy-two). This partly rounded off the edges of the sugar crystals. When made into candy, the resulting mixture had a silky way of melting that soon came to be considered the norm for all chocolate; the frequently used name "fondant" chocolate refers to this melting property.

Conched chocolate proved to be easier to use in baking. It had its oddities and tricks, which can still puzzle uninitiated cooks, but when handled correctly, it amalgamates smoothly and completely with cake batters, cookie and pastry dough, and custard mixtures. Plain ground chocolate was not sufficiently emulsified to do this. If you look at old cookbooks, you will notice that they contain very few recipes for chocolate in any but beverage form until about 1890 to 1900.

With these advances, chocolate could now be manufactured very cheaply on a huge industrial scale. It could be eaten—drinking chocolate had nearly disappeared except in the form of cocoa—by a cross-section of society from beggars to duchesses. Everyone became familiar with the faces of smiling children on the labels of favorite brands—Fry's or Cadbury's in England, Menier or Poulain in France, Lindt or Suchard in Switzerland, and later, Hershey in North America.

*Reméleuse, Moulage, Claquette,* 1870. This French print shows chocolate-making machines for mixing, molding, and vibrating molds to get rid of air bubbles.

## XOCOLAT FAMILIAR

A yellowing notebook dating from 1888 found at the old offices of Xocolat Arumi (today the Barcelona company Chocovic) contains recipes written in an elegant nineteenth-century hand, giving precise measurements for chocolate blends prepared specially for several local families. This was the so-called *xocolat familiar* (family-style chocolate). Some not only list flavorings—such as "Chinese" cinnamon (possibly cassia cinnamon) or pine nuts, a Catalan favorite—but also identify the type of cacao or blend of cacaos used in the recipe: Caracas or Guayaquil, or a mixture of the two. In these personalized recipes, we find the familiar hierarchy of quality and price.

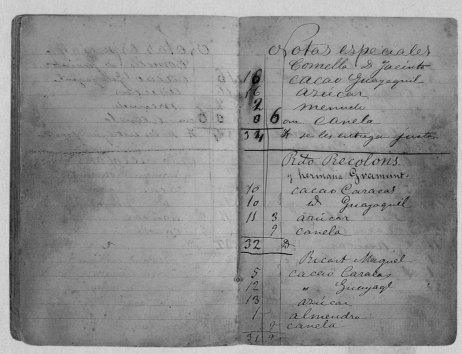

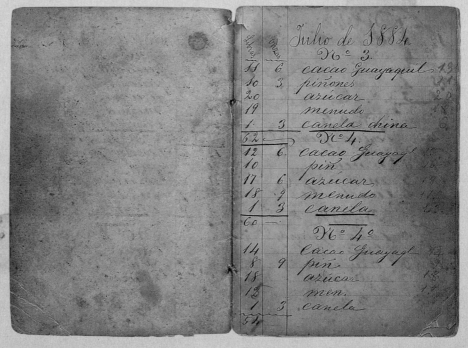

## Anonymous Chocolate

During the early industrial history of chocolate and way into the twentieth century, fine manufacturers continued using high-quality beans to produce their best chocolate blends. But the desire to create a uniform product that would carry their company's imprint, and the urge to keep their formulas secret, contributed to the divorce of chocolate from its place of origin. Even excellent chocolate had become faceless and anonymous, for the great majority of consumers now had no way of seeing and judging the cacao from which it was made. Only a scattering of small factories in Europe and Latin America kept alive the old customary ways of making chocolate.

As the price of chocolate went down, so did the quality of the cacao supply. The more careless manufacturers were happy to buy mixed batches of beans with scant regard to their quality. Overroasting and some conching often helped to reduce or mask the acidity and bitterness of cheap, unfermented *forastero* beans and create a more neutral-tasting end product that would reward a purchaser with exactly the same flavor and texture year in, year out. The practice of adding dried milk to the chocolate mass to make milk chocolate (a process introduced by the Swiss manufacturer Daniel Peter in 1879, the same year as Lindt's conching breakthrough) put another layer of distance between the consumer and the direct flavor of good and bad cacao.

## Cacao on the Move

*A new life had begun with the coming of cacao; what had happened earlier did not matter. Sugar mills and distilleries, plantations of sugar and coffee, old tales and legends, had disappeared forever. Now the groves of cacao were developing, and so were new stories of how men fought for possession of the land. The blind folk singers were carrying to the remotest country fairs the names and deeds of the men of cacao.*

JORGE AMADO, *GABRIELA, CLOVE AND CINNAMON*

Follow the equator, and you'll find cacao. Because of its particular climatic requirements, cacao was fated to become a Third World crop. Starting at the end of the seventeenth century, the Spanish carried it eastward to the Philippines, Java, and other islands of present-day Indonesia, and the Malay peninsula. The Portuguese made cacao-planting forays in some of the same areas. But their big contribution came in the nineteenth century when they conclusively established a Lower Amazon *forastero* from Bahia (Brazil) in West Africa, where the French also took up cacao cultivation. For a time, all the colonial powers (including the English, the Dutch, and even the Germans) sought to get a finger in the chocolate sauce.

All this activity had tremendous consequences. Once the European colonists in the New World became aware of the South American cacaos that would later be called "aliens," or *forasteros,* it was only a matter of time

1. Mexico, 2. Guatemala, 3. Honduras, 4. El Salvador, 5. Nicaragua, 6. Costa Rica, 7. Panama, 8. Colombia, 9. Ecuador, 10. Peru, 11. Bolivia, 12. Cuba, 13. Dominican Republic, 14. St. Lucia, 15. Grenada, 16. Trinidad, 17. Venezuela, 18. State of Pará (Brazil), 19. State of Bahia (Brazil), 20. Ivory Coast, 21. Ghana, 22. Togo, 23. Nigeria, 24. Cameroon, 25. Fernando Pó (Bioko), 26. Madagascar, 27. India, 28. Sri Lanka, 29. Java, 30. Malaysia, 31. Philippine Islands, 32. Sulawesi, 33. Papua New Guinea, 34. Solomon Islands, 35. Fiji, 36. Hawaii, 37. Samoa Islands. The red areas show cacao-producing regions.

Cacao did not stand still under the control of Spain and its rivals while chocolate was winning new converts. After establishing cacao plantations in the Caribbean, Spain tried to expand to other sites, hoping to corner the European market. But their ambitions were soon thwarted. Cacao trees require conditions like those found in their first American homes, and failed to produce even as far north of the equator as the tropic of Cancer or as far south as Capricorn.

before entrepreneurs would begin exploiting the enormous wild *forastero* reserves of the Amazon River basin and the northern Ecuadorian coast. By the end of the eighteenth century, the "new" cacao was on the move within the New World, and soon it would be on its way to Africa.

In the colonial and early modern era, the upper part of the Amazon River system had not been fully explored. The first wild cacaos discovered by settlers were the kind that grew along the lower Amazon. It was this prolific, hardy tree, called *amelonado* on account of its melon-shaped pods, that would facilitate an explosive nineteenth- and twentieth-century increase in the world supply of cacao.

The growth of the cacao industry brought thousands of Africans from Angola, the Congo area, Dahomey, and Calabar to Venezuela between the seventeenth and nineteenth centuries. Today their descendants tend the cacao farms and plantations of Barlovento and the coastal valleys of the state of Aragua. They are the heirs of the skills taught by the Spanish friars more than four centuries ago.

## WEST TO EAST, EAST TO WEST

The promise that speculators saw in cacao would transplant many thousands of Africans westward to Venezuela, Ecuador, Brazil, and the Caribbean islands and East Indians to islands like Trinidad. It would draw smaller numbers of Europeans in the same direction to seek their fortunes as landowners, farm supervisors, or merchants. French planters coming from Haiti settled in Trinidad after the Haitian revolution at the end of the eighteenth century. They were followed in the nineteenth century by Corsicans who also settled in the Paria Peninsula in Venezuela.

The cacao boom also sent cacao traveling the other way across the Atlantic and put down millions of trees in the regions that are modern-day Nigeria, Ghana, Cameroon, and the Ivory Coast. It scattered vast plantations tended by slaves (or after emancipation, day laborers or tenant farmers) over millions of acres of tropical forest. It also poised the economic survival of large regions or whole countries on the steadily narrowing genetic base of one plant species.

For some reason, Brazil initially lagged behind the Spanish colonies in promoting cacao culture, to which it gave an official blessing only in 1679. But in 1746 the French settler Luiz Frederico Warneau transplanted some cacao seedlings—though only as ornamentals—from Pará to a plantation on the River Pardo, not far south of Ilhéus on the east coast of today's state of Bahia. It proved to be a fruitful environment for growing cacao. At that time Bahia was sugar country, one of the major destinations of the slave ships. But the new European chocolate technology starting with Van Houten's cocoa process in 1828 signaled golden opportunities for expansion in Bahia. A ragtag wave of workers poured in from all over Brazil. Soon *amelonado* cacao (locally called "Brazil *comum*") replaced sugar as the region's leading source of wealth. By 1906, Brazil—

In the nineteenth century, Corsicans settled in Trinidad and the nearby Paria Peninsula, in Venezuela, where they became landowners and farm supervisors. Arsenio Borthomierth, the second-generation Corsican who manages La Concepción farm in Barlovento, Venezuela, proudly holds a *criollo* pod.

THE NEW TASTE OF CHOCOLATE

mostly meaning Bahia—was the world's greatest cacao producer.

At the same time, *amelonado*-type cacao was being planted in most of the Caribbean sugar dominions. In the late nineteenth century, it began its rise to the great cash crop of West Africa.

Aside from the special case of Venezuela, there are a few areas of the cacao-growing world where *forastero* did not come to dominate the industry. The trees that the Spanish first brought to the Philippines were *criollos,* and as cacao spread westward to Indonesia and Malaysia, *criollo* was the foundation of the first plantations (though profit-minded growers later brought in *trinitarios* and various hybrids, followed in the second half of the twentieth century by *amelonados*). A major factor in keeping *criollo* afloat in this part of the world after *forasteros* had come to the forefront elsewhere was the growth of the milk chocolate industry. *Trinitario* cacao brought to the island of Java from Venezuela was bred with the island's *criollo* cacao and evolved into a strain famous for the attractive light color of the beans even after roasting, a marked cosmetic advantage in the finished product.

The other anomaly in the story of the global takeover of Lower Amazon *forastero* is Ecuador. Geneticists conjecture that it was home to some singular cacao strains long before the Spanish colonial period. As the Venezuelan cacao growers' share of the enterprise declined around the turn of the nineteenth century, Ecuador charged in to flood the market with a lesser-quality cacao. To dealers, it was known as "Guayaquil cacao"

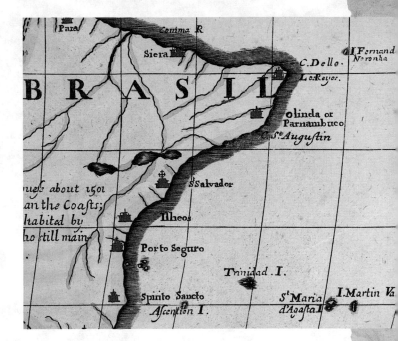

Bahia from *A New Map of South America, Showing Its General Divisions, Chief Cities & Towns, Rivers, Mountains, & Dedicated to His Highness William Duke of Gloucester* by Wells, Oxford, 1700. From the late nineteenth century until recent outbreaks of witches' broom disease, the Brazilian state of Bahia was the largest cacao-growing region in Latin America.

after the port from which it was shipped, but its popular nickname was "poor people's cacao." But other genetic material was already in Ecuador—a *criollo* or a hybrid from Trinidad, generically called "Criollo from Venezuela," that had crossed with Ecuador's native *Nacional* cacao. These hybrids produced a better cacao, which was sold under the umbrella name of "Esmeralda," after the humid northern province where it was grown. Another region of Ecuador on the upper Guayas River became known for another of the

East Indian workers in Trinidad get ready for the cacao harvest. The men hold long poles fitted with sharp blades for picking cacao.

plant's still unplumbed genetic mysteries: Arriba, a unique type of *Nacional* cacao. It is a *forastero* with good basic flavor and a distinctive flowery bouquet that people in the chocolate business can recognize immediately.

Descendants of the first *trinitarios* and a wide array of other *forastero-criollo* hybrids continued to be fitfully explored wherever growers wanted to upgrade the flavor of their cacao. Yet the overall *criollo* element on the world's cacao plantations has been shrinking from disease and neglect for close to two hundred years. With a few exceptions, *criollo* cacao all but disappeared from its old Mexican and Central American strongholds, replaced by plantings of *forastero* that the growers considered hardier. Some Mexican plantations in Chiapas state have a few *criollo* trees. In the area of Chinandega in Nicaragua, there are still pockets of a fine *criollo* strain formerly called "royal cacao" or *cacao real.* This cacao is known for its large warty, red pods with curved pointy tips, which are probably identical to the remaining *criollos* growing in the central coastal valleys of Venezuela. In 1995, a team of scientists from the Smithsonian and Trinidad's Cocoa Research Unit discovered scattered *criollo* trees growing wild in the mountains of Belize, probably relics of Mayan times. Previous expeditions had also found isolated wild *criollo* trees in Mayan "sacred groves" in the Yucatan and in the Lacandon forest in eastern Chiapas. But only in Venezuela did a large spectrum of *criollo* cacao and hybrids with high-*criollo* germplasm manage to survive. This is why Venezuelan cacao never lost its special reputation among dealers and chocolatiers who knew quality.

THE NEW TASTE OF CHOCOLATE

## DISEASE: THE ACHILLES HEEL

Unfortunately for everyone from cacao dealers to peasants in the new domains of *forastero,* the supposedly hardy trees of the Lower Amazon proved to be vulnerable to disease. Wherever large plantings were made, sooner or later a pest or disease would appear that would wipe out a crop within days or cripple a whole plantation within a year or two. Some scourges would make their way from one established growing region to neighboring ones. Others occurred in new regions where cacao turned out to present a virgin target to some local virus, fungus, or insect.

Names like "witches' broom," "capsid," "swollen shoot," "black pod rot," and "cocoa wilt" came to strike terror into entire communities or nations. The vagaries of weather—capable of creating disaster in their own right—could also create new opportunities for disease or threaten the lives of the all-important shade trees. A seemingly innocent plant like the Amazonian *cupuaçu* or the African kola tree might turn out to be a host for one of cacao's many emerging enemies. Considering what a harsh mistress cacao could be, it is not surprising that eventually the great estates of the colonial period began to be broken up. In most of the world's cacao regions only small farmers remained to tend the chancy crop on tiny plots of ground with little between them and ruin.

Around the turn of the twentieth century, cacao-growing nations and major chocolate companies began to apply scientific methods to the problems of cacao, and the study of varieties evolved into a precise search for the most highly productive, disease-resistant cacaos. The early twentieth century saw the founding of research centers and experimental stations, of which the Imperial College of Tropical Agriculture (today a part of the University of the West Indies) on Trinidad soon became the greatest. It was at this point that the Upper Amazon *forastero* strains entered the commercial picture.

The first record of cultivated cacao in Indonesia dates from 1778. Presumably *criollo* cacao had arrived in Java from the Philippines at an earlier date. However, the genotype that produces the coveted bean known to the trade as Java A or fine *("edel")* cacao is technically a *trinitario*—the progeny of Java's native *criollo* population and a single Venezuelan *trinitario* tree brought to the island in 1888 and planted in Djati Roenggo estate.

By now, the technique of cloning the best stock was being practiced on some advanced plantations on a large scale. In the late 1930s, geneticist F. J. Pound of the Imperial College of Tropical Agriculture on Trinidad began a series of cacao-collecting expeditions—later continued by others—among the wild stands of *forastero* cacao trees along the western Amazon and its tributaries coming down from the Andes in Peru and Ecuador. Their hope was to infuse new blood, or at any rate new genes, into the vulnerable cacao supply. Over a period of decades, scientists from the Imperial College of Tropical Agriculture planted seedlings from chosen specimens on several farms, among them Marper Farm, which today stands as a relic of Trinidad's pioneering effort against cacao diseases. The likeliest candidates were cloned and crossed with each other as well as with select *trinitario* cultivars (selected from the best original *trinitario* population of the island). The most successful resulting trees were cloned for commercial distribution. The criteria of success were simple: high yields and immunity to disease and pests.

The field of cacao research blossomed. In cacao-growing nations around the world, government- or industry-sponsored research

Plant pathologist Jean-Marc Thévenin examines a dried-out witches' broom sample at the pathology laboratory of the Cocoa Research Unit.

LEFT: *Crinipella perniciosa,* the pathogen responsible for the dreaded witches' broom disease, has a complex life cycle. When the fungus first infects a cacao tree, it lives between the cells of the plant and causes abnormal growth of the infected area. In most cases, the tree will put forth a flush of seemingly healthy new leaves. But when the fungus invades the cells of the plant and kills them, it enters a saprophytic phase during which it receives nourishment from the plant's dead tissue. After six to seven weeks, the flush of leaves shrivels and dies out, resembling a broom.

THE NEW TASTE OF CHOCOLATE

Members of the 1952–53 Anglo-Colombian cacao collection expedition to the Colombian Amazon

facilities began studying the potential of the Trinidadian clones and Trinidad Select Hybrids (TSH) and advising farmers on their use. One of the most dramatic results was a second movement of cacao germplasm around the globe. This time the germplasm came from Upper Amazon strains and the so-called Ecuadorian *refractarios* (Ecuadorian *forasteros* chosen for their apparent immunity to disease) and circulated with greater efficiency and knowledge. The overall share of *criollo* in the world supply dwindled even further. Yet the long-term consequences of this "new" germplasm were no miracle. For many decades the last thing the researchers (and most growers) thought of was what kind of chocolate the new cacao cultivars would make—some of the disease-resistant plants produced acid and bitter tasting chocolate. Moreover, the very efficiency of modern breeding and cloning programs turned out to be

a mixed blessing. It rapidly caused the genetic basis of commercial cacao, already narrowed through long reliance on *amelonado* types, to shrink still more. After a few generations, farms planted with many clones of a few alleged wonder stocks proved more susceptible than anyone had guessed to new troubles and diseases—and some of the old ones as well.

The last decades have been catastrophic ones in some of the world's most fruitful regions. The Bahian plantations are close to ruin, decimated by witches' broom. Ecuador's cacao industry has been collapsing throughout the twentieth century. Its prized Arriba, already in serious trouble, received what may have been the coup de grâce from the 1982 to 1983 and the 1997 to 1998 climatic disruptions of El Niño. (Already in 1937, F. J. Pound had reported that this valued strain showed little real resistance to witches' broom disease.)

*Metamorphosis Insectorum Surinamensium* by Maria Sibylla Merian, 1705. This copper engraving shows cacao pods from the Dutch Guyana

Cacao

## The Promise of Cacao

Given the dire circumstances of cacao today, it may seem perverse of me to describe this as a time of immense hope and promise, but in many ways it is. Several factors are contributing to the writing of an epochal chapter in the history of chocolate.

The first is DNA analysis and genome mapping. For the first time we have the realistic prospect of being able to identify the genes responsible for precise traits in cacao (and the chocolate made from it), and also to trace just where and how the different *criollo* and *forastero* strains split off from some ancestral *Theobroma* and from each other. We are in a position to study the makeup of cacao's wild *Theobroma* cousins and perhaps adapt some of their survival strategies to combat the cultivated plant's natural enemies.

Allied with this effort are pioneering studies of tropical ecosystems and the environmental adaptability of cacao. We are starting to learn more about the interrelationships among organisms (for example, the best insect pollinators for low-yielding strains). On experimental and some commercial farms, growers have found that cacao can be raised successfully on open ground with little shade as long as it is well irrigated—a discovery that might be of important consequence in opening up new cultivation areas.

Deforestation in areas where cacao originated threatens to destroy the genetic diversity of this marvelous plant. It is encouraging to see that concern over the genetic erosion of cacao has led to its designation as a priority crop for conservation. At the heart of the effort to conserve cacao's biodiversity is the creation of germplasm banks—safe havens for wild varieties of cacao that are now threatened.

The very term "germplasm bank" conjures up a world of test tubes. But a cacao germplasm bank is, really, halfway between a large plantation and a botanical garden. There scientists and agronomists keep thousands of cacao trees (domesticated and wild) from all over the world, for conservation, research, and use in plant-breeding programs.

Most cacao-producing countries have their own limited germplasm banks, but only the International Cocoa Genebank of Trinidad (ICG, T) and the Centro Agronómico Tropical de Investigaciones y Enseñanza (CATIE) in Turrialba, Costa Rica, have been designated as universal collection depositories. Of the two, Trinidad has the largest number of accessions (close to three thousand).

The most encouraging sign that we are about to enter into a new era for cacao is that the major research institutes have now had their eyes opened to the importance of fine cacao flavor as a breeding criterion. Part of the training programs for cacao researchers and agronomists now involves learning to recognize the best-tasting specimens and to select them for reproduction with the goal of excellence clearly in mind.

Yet for all the present possibilities and future advances, nothing can ever eliminate the risks, uncertainties, and infinite labor of actual cacao farming. It will always be at least as much an art as a science, and all chocolate lovers should understand what is involved.

# From Cacao to Chocolate

Imagine walking through an orchard unlike any other you have ever seen—a jumbled community of trees, vines, and other growth shrouded in the sweltering green chiaroscuro of the South American lowlands. The air is close and humid; the silence is broken only by the hum of insects and the crackle of dead leaves underfoot. The vengeful sunlight of the tropics pierces the great canopy of towering shade trees, slivering into a thousand rays as it hits the leaves of other small, slender trees around you in the dusky understory. These graceful trees, bearing fruit the size of footballs that grow straight out of lichen-spotted, gray-brown trunks, are the real heart of this unlikely orchard. This is cacao, the source of every chocolate bar and truffle ever made. The sight is somehow primeval, atavistic, like something you would expect in a Jurassic jungle. You begin to look for dinosaurs lurking in the dark recesses of this old cacao plantation. No kind of growth seems impossible in the garden of chocolate.

A cacao plantation is a hothouse without glass, a place of wanton promiscuity where slender tree trunks bear weighty fruits like the pendulous breasts of a tropical fertility goddess. The cacao pods thrive in the steamy heat, presenting an incredible wealth of colors, shapes, and surface textures. An evergreen without a distinct harvest season, the cacao tree puts forth flowers continuously. So, at any one moment, you see Lilliputian flowers next to Gulliver-sized fruits, from the tiny gherkin-shaped baby fruits to toddler specimens like small eggplants and adolescent-sized specimens as big as half-grown spaghetti squashes—all in a range of colors that at first seems random. During peaks of growth, the huge multi-

ABOVE: Chocolate in a concher

OPPOSITE: Cacao workers in Barlovento, Venezuela

colored pods look like parrots and macaws perching on the trees. Even when fully mature, the pods can range from bright green to pale yellow, dark purple to burnt orange or crimson. What makes the sight so amazing is that even at the same stage of growth, two fruits on the same tree may be very different shades. Some seem to be sculpted with ridges, furrows, craters, or warts; others are smooth and shiny as if enameled or rough-skinned and dappled with dark spots. Some have meandering lines over the surface, perhaps traced by insects or other creatures. The shapes are as startling as the colors. A cacao fruit can be as round as a melon or as long as an enormous teardrop. At the stem end, it can have a pronounced bottleneck or none at all. At the other end, it can be pointed, smooth, or indented.

Alongside the luscious ripening fruits hang the remains of others that have withered on the tree. Cacao fruits refuse to let go of the mother tree even when they have died.

## Logical Green Anarchy

To a first-time visitor, a traditional cacao plantation always looks like green anarchy. But for those who work there, it is supremely logical. The skills of the farm workers who maintain the cacao trees and their complex environments are highly developed. This knowledge is usually passed on from generation to generation.

The farms I know most intimately are in the New World. But the same planting and caretaking needs exist wherever cacao is grown and are fulfilled in mostly very similar ways. In traditional farming, the first requirements are shade and water. Shade keeps the leaves from being burned and the soil from being baked and eroded. A good year-round supply of water is also needed, but preferably with adequate soil drainage and no long periods of flooding. On most new farms today, water for irrigation is piped to the trees from wells or streams and delivered by a drip method. On older farms, the ground on which the trees are planted is often divided into islands by irrigation ditches that workers have to cross to get to their jobs.

But whether or not such visible boundary lines exist, plantations are generally organized

LEFT: At the Estación Experimental Chama in the state of Zulia, Venezuela, sectors of pure *porcelana* cacao are divided by wide irrigation ditches.

OPPOSITE: Guasare cacao, a pure *criollo,* thrives at the experimental farm of San Juan de Lagunillas in the Venezuelan Andes. This precocious three-year-old Guasare tree is being irrigated by the drip method.

At present most of the world's cacao farms have no substitute for the skills of families with deep roots in a plantation; little can be mechanized. The cacao tree does best in a traditional tropical farm setting where a sizable force of highly experienced workers can give constant attention to a complex polyculture every month of the year.

into "sectors," which may range in size from a few acres to a hundred acres or more. From Spanish colonial times, the sector (in parts of Venezuela known as *ahilado*) has been the basic unit of responsibility, farmed by a small team of workers—usually a family with roots on the plantation.

## CHOREOGRAPHING LIFE

A farmer's duties begin not only with planting the cacao trees but also with choreographing their surroundings. Some plots simply make use of existing forest cover, but there comes a time when new cover trees have to be created from scratch. To begin a new plot, the workers must stagger the growth of the shade trees to have them ready at the right time. They plant small leafy trees, such as yuca (cassava) or coffee bush and plantain or banana trees, so that the first-stage shade will be in place when the cacao starts growing. Meanwhile, they also plant fast-growing upper-story trees that will reach their full growth when the cacao is ready to bear.

The choice of shade trees can be pretty wide. Plantains and bananas are popular everywhere for the early shade. The upper-story trees can be coconut palms (especially in Southeast Asia), kola-nut trees in Africa (though unfortunately they carry cacao diseases), rubber, or mango. Among Latin American favorites are mahogany, or *caoba (Swietenia mahogani); bucare (Erythrina velutina* or *E. poeppigiana);* and the very tall, spectacularly dense and spreading *gran samán* or raintree *(Pithecellobium saman).*

The mix of smaller and larger shade trees, along with many vines and climbing plants springing up in the same space, supports a complex of insect life that helps pollinate the cacao trees and other plants. That is why I consider cacao such a life-giving crop above and beyond the pleasure we take in chocolate— cacao is an intrinsic protector of the environment.

The cacao trees that are planted in each new sector usually are not randomly chosen. The workers already know which of the existing trees in other parts of the farm are the best bearers and try to retain seeds from their pods when the cacao is harvested. The beans will be planted in a nursery area that may also have slips or buds propagated from some desired stock through cloning (that is, removing them from the parent tree and grafting them onto other rootstock). The young plants are ready to be transplanted into the prepared ground in a worker's assigned sector when they are slightly bigger than knee high, at about four or five months.

Once established in its sector, a cacao tree usually takes about four years to start bearing, though some varieties are ready at three, or even two. In the meantime, the workers carefully remove any suckers (*chupones* in Spanish) that might drain off energy from the main growth. They prune the trees to a compact shape that will concentrate the flowers and fruit on the trunk and lower parts of the main branches, an important advantage for later harvesting. By

Flowering *bucares* tower over a mixed-growth farm in the Venezuelan Andes.

vigilant pruning, the trees are kept to a standard height of about 20 feet (about 6 meters, half the height of the tallest cacao trees in nature). But the current fashion is for even more severe dwarfing to permit the trees to be planted as densely as 40 inches (about 1 meter) apart.

A cacao seedling will grow fairly straight up to the first branching; a grafted tree generally puts forth spreading boles. While the young trees grow, the workers watch for signs of disease, periodically clear the undergrowth enough to keep the trees accessible, and also manage the edible crops produced by some of the shade trees (yuca and plantains).

## BLOSSOMING AND BEARING

When the tree is between two and four years old, the first diminutive orchidlike cacao blossoms will sprout on tiny stems that stick straight out of scattered cushionlike patches on the trunk (literally down to the ground) and the lowest branches. The flowers are white, varying to whitish pink or whitish yellow (according to individual strain) and not much bigger than tomato blossoms. They have five arrow-shaped petals set around an intricate sheathing of stamens and pistils.

The cacao tree is an indeterminate blossomer, putting forth new flowers year-round

A typical nursery for cacao seedlings, at the Estación Experimental Chama, a propagation center for pure *porcelana* cacao in the humid flatlands south of Lake Maracaibo. The nursery workers first loosen the seeds from the mucilaginous pulp of the pods, then plant them, individually enclosed in sturdy polyethylene bags, in rich organic soil. Dark netting protects the delicate seedlings from direct sunlight.

THE NEW TASTE OF CHOCOLATE

with one or two strong peaks per year (according to region), the profligacy of blooms offsetting the amazingly low fertility of cacao flowers. They are so difficult to pollinate successfully that of the many thousand flowers on a mature tree, only about one hundred will survive to become pods in a year.

Once a blossom is successfully pollinated, it takes about five to six months to become a mature fruit. The farmers must keep track of each one as it approaches ripeness. About a month after pollination, a gherkin-sized baby pod, called a *chirel* (in Spanish) or *cherelle* (in French), develops on the short blossom stem. When it is fully grown, it will be from nine to thirteen inches long and can weigh up to about a pound. The shape depends on the ancestry of the cacao. Since the colors vary wildly, experienced judgment is needed to know when a green, yellow, or dark purple fruit is ready to be harvested. The harvest season varies from region to region, depending on local rainfall patterns.

Baby cacao pods

On a cacao tree, diminutive orchidlike blossoms and tiny fruits hang right next to mature pods.

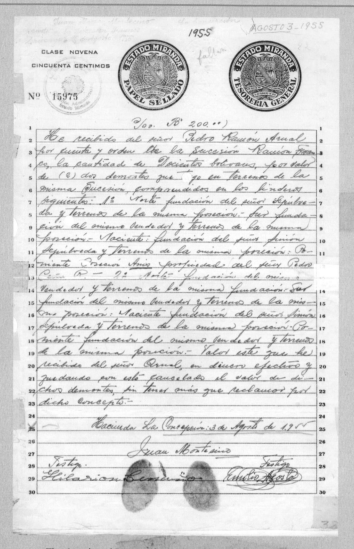

*The Arnal and Duarte dispute and hundreds of other planta-tion minutiae were meticulously recorded in the clear hand of notaries at the municipal court of neighboring El Clavo. Looking at the polite formalities of the document, we might suppose we were observing transactions between social equals. But then some jarring reminder of the deep social divide between the landowning classes and the people who grew cacao for them emerges in the form of a thumbprint (in lieu of a signature) on a lease or some mention of a farmer's inability to read and write.*

## THE BIRTH OF A CACAO PLANTATION

Latin American cacao plantations came into being over the centuries by varied local paths. The 870-acre (352 hectare) Hacienda La Concepción in the north-ern Venezuelan region of Barlovento typifies a system that is somewhat like Southern sharecropping in the United States. It probably arose for the same reason, when many thousands of ex-slaves were left to fend for themselves after the abolition of slavery in 1854. The hacienda's records are preserved to this day and provide a window into the everyday life of an early modern plantation.

La Concepción's founder was a planter named Ramón Franco, who started acquiring property in the area about one generation after emancipation. Franco then leased the land to an assemblage of tenants, mostly of African descent, who did the actual farming. An average initial lease seems to have been for five years. As in most of the Barlovento plantations, the agreement was that each tenant was in charge of clearing a designated area or areas at his own expense. In these parts, such plots were generally called *ahilados*, a term that roughly translates into "lined-up files"—that is, rows of trees. They must have varied greatly in acreage, since the records refer to wildly disparate numbers of trees in different *ahilados*.

In every *ahilado*, it was the tenant's job to get the primary and secondary shade trees in place before planting the cacao. Each *ahilado* had its own nursery, or *almácigo*, where cacao was grown directly from seed under the shade of a breadfruit tree. At about five months, the seedlings were transplanted to their permanent spots, lined up in the carefully spaced files to which the term *ahilado* refers.

Most of the early documents concern the rever-sion of *ahilados* to the landlord, Franco, on the expira-tion of the initial leases. Up to that point, while the trees were growing, and probably before they were bearing, the tenants were allowed to keep and presumably sell any cacao they harvested. The farmers were then entitled to some compensation for the addition to the value of the land. What they received seems to have depended on the number of cacao trees planted in the unit.

Once the trees were producing fully and the first lease was up, another system of arrangement called *medianería* began. The tenant became a *medianero*, who supplied the landlord with a set number of kilos yearly (usually half the cacao crop) or the equivalent monetary value according to the going price of cacao in neighboring towns, and who retained some interest in the cacao trees he or she had originally planted.

That the life of the *medianero* was not an easy one is shown by a series of 1940s documents recording a dispute between Pedro Ramón Arnal, the foreman of La Concepción, and a tenant farmer named Quirino Olegario Duarte. Duarte had failed to come up with the 250 kilos of "good cacao in good condition" stipulated in his contract because his cacao trees still were not bearing. This skirmish between Arnal and Duarte became an ongoing saga. Years later we find Duarte back in court. The dispute was temporarily resolved when Arnal allowed the tenant to remain on his land "two years longer so that he can continue caring for the cacao trees."

After Ramón Franco died in 1921, his children long remained in possession of the farm. Over time, cacao underwent a general decline in Barlovento, and at La Concepción, as at many other plantations, the land was neglected or half abandoned. In some places, the tenant farmers took over or obtained titles to the patches of ground they had been tending for years. This is the origin of the thousands of tiny cacao farms (less than about twelve acres) in Barlovento today.

In 1993 new owners bent on revitalization—Silvino Reyes and his wife, Ana Karina Flores—took over La Concepción and started the difficult process of bringing it back to life, *ahilado* by *ahilado*. Today La Concepción is once again a vigorous plantation of forty-seven *ahilados* laid out with the same spacing of trees that the first farmers established. It is a wonderful union of tradition and technology.

While Arsenio Borthomierth, a Venezuelan of Corsican blood who has lived with cacao all his life, studies the phases of the moon to decide how to schedule the pruning of the large shade trees, Silvino Reyes is busy figuring out how to make the fermentation facility more efficient and installing the region's only device for polishing the treated beans, as is sometimes done in Trinidad. And when they discuss their daily routine, they allude to the names of the original *ahilados,* as if the spirits of the first owners and tenant farmers lived on in these lots of Venezuelan earth.

La Concepción today

## TENDING AND HARVESTING

In all cacao-growing regions various family members share in the work. In the central coastal valleys of Venezuela, the men do the clearing and heavy cutting in each sector while women tend and harvest the fruit. The worker goes out daily to the assigned sector with a machete and a sharp blade fixed on a long pole. The trick is to sever the stem and retrieve the heavy pod without disturbing the cushionlike area that it grows from, and without damaging any flowers or immature fruits. The pods are cut open to remove the seeds and the sticky, sweet-tart pulp that surrounds them. On some plantations, the harvester does this on the spot, right under the trees, and then carries the beans in a basket lined with plantain leaves to a central location. There she will dump the cacao beans in a heap, coming back and forth several times over the course of the day until she has checked all her assigned trees. Only then will she start carrying the beans back to the farmhouse to be weighed. On other farms, the unopened pods may be carried on somebody's back or head (or via mules or horses) to a central location. There another woman waits to split them open.

Back at the farmhouse, the baskets are weighed. Harvesters are normally paid by the weight of the wet, freshly harvested cacao in its surrounding pulp, technically, *cacao en baba* (from the Spanish *baba,* or "slime"). Once the beans are collected, the cycle of growth and harvest is complete.

Cacao goes on bearing without interruption until it reaches the end of its life. Most trees peak when they about seven years old, but can continue producing well for another fifteen to twenty years. Some are still producing good crops when they reach fifty to seventy-five years of age. But generally the trees of a given sector are replaced long before this. In progressive plantations, a veteran plantation manager or skilled technician usually replaces the older trees with cloned (budded or grafted) stock rather than seedlings. This ensures a high degree of uniformity in the tree's performance. An entire sector may be planted with clones from a single strain that is developed on a specific plantation or at one of the world's great germplasm banks and is known to possess fine flavor or resistance to a particular disease.

Virgilia Córdoba has spent all of her life working as a cacao harvester in Barlovento, Venezuela.

# Cacao-to-Chocolate Alchemy

All cacao farming closely follows a similar routine up to the moment when someone cleaves open the pods and disembowels them. This takes great skill and strength; the rind of the fruit in some *forasteros* can be extremely hard to cut through cleanly, and it is easy to slice into the beans.

## FERMENTING

In the best South American cacao farms, an important role is played by the glistening white fruit pulp, or *baba,* that surrounds the almond-like beans. The sticky mass is first cleaned of foreign objects, pieces of rind, and fibrous placenta. Then workers heap it in wooden bins and cover it with plantain leaves to begin fermentation.

The rich complement of sugars in the sweet-tart *baba* starts fermenting at once, eventually turning into acetic acid (the main component of vinegar). The temperature of the mass rises while the pH goes down, which cause the hulls and the germ tip to soften and allow the acid to penetrate. These factors together kill the germ or embryo within the bean. Meanwhile, the semisolid *baba* spontaneously melts into a liquid vinegar that drains off of its own accord to leave the slightly darkened beans free, though still full of moisture.

The death of the embryo is like turning off an override switch—it allows the bean to rush into another mode, launching a complex sequence of chemical processes like a tiny factory. Some of the sour, bitter, and astringent compounds within the beans (organic acids, anthocyanins, tannins, catechins) pass through the now permeable skins, eliminating the harsher flavors. Some begin to transform into mellower substances by the action of enzymes.

The length of the fermentation process depends on the variety of cacao: the best *criollos* need as little as forty-eight hours and the other cacaos about six or more days. The beans are rotated from one bin to another to promote the aeration of the fermenting mass. The proper degree of fermentation is determined by cutting some beans open and checking to see if the cotyledons are wrinkled.

Box fermentation at Hacienda La Concepción in Barlovento, Venezuela. A worker arranges plantain leaves over a large "sweating" box filled to capacity with *cacao en baba,* to promote yeast and bacterial activity during fermentation. The beans are mixed and turned from box to box three or four times during the fermentation period.

## DRYING

When fermentation is completed, the beans are removed from the fermenting bin and spread in the sun to dry on the cement floor of a drying patio or on large, wide wooden shelves or platforms. During this period they are periodically turned with wooden rakes. At night they are pulled into sheds for protection or covered by clear plastic roofing materials. In about five to six days, the chemical changes within the beans gradually slow down and then stop when the moisture content has dropped to less than 8 percent by weight.

Workers then take a sample of one hundred beans and perform a cut test to make sure they are perfectly dried before removing them from the drying yard. Only then are the beans transferred to a storage room where they are usually heaped against a wall. As the beans accumulate, workers shovel them often to facilitate aeration and to prevent molding. At the peak of the harvest, the pile of beans can easily reach the storage room ceiling.

The beans are now hard, dry, and somewhat shrunken. They have acquired a new name in Spanish-speaking countries: *almendras,* or almonds. Up to this point they have been known as *semillas,* or seeds. For the first-quality *criollo* and *trinitario* cacaos grown on the premier farms, the interior color, which began as white or very light purple and changed to yellowish brown during fermentation, is now medium brown. *Forastero* cacao will have turned from purple to dark brown.

On the island of Grenada, as in parts of Venezuela, coffee and cacao are sundried on large paved patios adjacent to the curing (fermentation) houses, as shown in this print from about 1857.

THE NEW TASTE OF CHOCOLATE

Alexander Fariñas, a worker at Hacienda La Concepción, turns cacao beans with a wooden rake several times a day to ensure that they are evenly sundried.

The underpinnings of chocolate flavor are now in place (though you wouldn't find them fully developed if you ate a bean at this stage).

At least up to the eighteenth century, most Latin American plantations from Mexico to northern South America grew delicately flavored *criollo* varieties of cacao, which require only light fermentation to develop a rich chocolate flavor and aroma. When the cacao in commercial plantations became mostly *forastero* or a mixed batch, the whole equation changed. Those people who choose a short fermentation period or none at all for such cacao are helping to produce bitter, astringent, and overly acid cacao beans. Those who ferment for

an extended period can tame the harshness of *forastero*. But unfortunately many cacao processors have no choice but to mingle beans of different origins in the fermenting bins—their plantations are a genetic mosaic. Only with constant care of the fermenting mass can they reach a comfortable middle ground to keep the better beans *(criollos* and *trinitarios)* from overfermenting and developing off-flavors, or the cheap ones *(forasteros)* from being underfermented and acidic. This explains why it is not uncommon to find partially fermented purple beans in a batch of fine *trinitario* beans. In some producing countries like Malaysia, it has been found that the flavor of cacao can be improved and high acidity and astringency reduced by the simple post-harvest technique of leaving the pods unopened for several days. Also, where a uniform, fairly homogeneous *forastero* crop has been grown with care—for example, the sturdy, dependable *amelonado* cacao of Ghana—experienced farmers can ferment it for reliable chocolate flavor.

A cut test ensures proper drying for the cacao beans.

Yanomami women wash freshly harvested cacao beans to extract the pulp at the Venezuelan community of Washewe on the Mavaca River in the Upper Orinoco Basin.

## BUILDING LAYERS OF FLAVOR AND AROMA

If you were to line up and taste two dozen finished chocolate samples from as many manufacturers, the variations you would find—aside from the innate differences among *criollos, forasteros,* and hybrids—would overwhelmingly reflect what had been done during fermentation and drying.

Extensive, well-developed fermentation may well have been a Spanish contribution. Whether the first colonists found the Mexicans fully fermenting cacao beans *en baba,* or simply rinsing the pulp after a very short sweating, may never be known. Some peoples of Latin America today, like most farmers in Tabasco, Mexico, and some Amazon and Orinoco region Indians, simply rinse the pulp.

Without the help of the sugar-rich pulp, their cacao does not have a chance to ferment even partially when drying. The result is aspirin-bitter beans. In many parts of Latin America, the beans are simply spread to dry on any flat surface after being extracted from the pod. When this is done, the beans experience a partial fermentation, which is better than none at all.

# The Cacao Trade

After the beans have been fermented and dried, they are classified according to size. For this, most plantations I have seen use creaky turn-of-the-century European sorting machines that look like ancient drums. They still do their job to perfection. This is an important moment in the life of chocolate. The trade classifies beans according to size and quality. Only specialty or high-quality beans are sold at premium prices. The assorted beans are then placed in burlap bags and weighed.

A complex web of buyers and intermediaries is behind every bag of cacao that leaves its place of origin. Because cacao is produced in Third World countries with no tradition of large industrial chocolate manufacturing, the best cacao is exported. The rest is used by local manufacturers or by artisanal producers. In Latin America, only Venezuela has a modern European-style chocolate company of world distinction (owned by Venezuelans) that uses 100 percent premium Venezuelan cacao and processes it with state-of-the-art European technology.

Most chocolate companies prefer to use brokers to buy the raw material. From glistening offices in London, New York, and Amsterdam, these brokers act as intermediaries between producers or local brokers and the manufacturers.

LEFT: At La Reunión, a government-run plantation in Trinidad, dried cacao beans are classified according to size using a nineteenth-century sorting machine.
ABOVE: After being dried and classified, cacao beans are placed in burlap bags and weighed according to each producing country's regulations.

In a single day, a busy New York cacao broker working for a large international firm will deal by phone and fax with as many as twenty cacao-producing countries around the world to discuss prices, draw contracts, and arrange shipments. Both brokers and chocolate manufacturers require samples of any lot of beans before shipping or upon arrival. Buyers reserve the right to turn down any shipment on the basis of a sample test.

Cacao prices are futures commodity prices per metric ton set by the New York or London stock exchange. In the late 1990s, prices plummeted to an all-time low, though individual producers or countries were sometimes able to charge a premium for superior quality beans way above market price. Some countries—for example, Trinidad—choose to set their own prices independent of the vagaries of the stock exchange.

## PERILOUS JOURNEYS

The life of the cacao bean is perilous from beginning to end. Each step cacao takes toward the chocolate factory has a bearing on the ultimate quality of the final product. International trade regulations as well as strict sanitary protection laws by each importing country require that the bags be sprayed before being shipped and upon arrival at its destination. This is meant to control parasites, moths, and other stowaway critters. Humidity control during shipping is also essential for quality. Most cacao beans travel around the world for months in the bowels of large ships before reaching the factory. This is an expensive proposition, for long voyages require ventilated storage containers. Upon reception at the factory or broker's warehouse, the bags are fumigated again and ideally stored in temperature-controlled rooms. Other challenges await the beans at the factory.

## PASSING THE QUALITY TEST

Every lot of cacao that makes it to the factory is examined carefully. Expert chocolatiers take random samples of three hundred beans per each metric ton of cacao and separate them into three groups of one hundred each. After weighing one hundred beans to estimate bean size, the company cuts all the beans lengthwise, revealing the open cotyledons, to look for insect activity, flat beans, clustered beans, and mold, and to determine the degree of fermentation. The trade classifies beans as "slaty" when the cut cotyledons look flat and compact, with none of the characteristic open kidneylike structure and light break of the well-fermented bean. Each company has a different protocol with regard to the percentage of defects allowed in a single sampling.

The technical staff of any chocolate company make routine laboratory samples of cacao liquor from each lot for sensory evaluation. Each company appoints a panel of expert tasters whose job is to sample cacao liquors almost on a daily basis. Silvio Crespo, formerly a technical director for several chocolate companies, says that he used to eat a pound of chocolate a day (counting both liquor and finished chocolate).

Liquor tasting is not the same as chocolate tasting. Tasters must concentrate on the intrinsic flavor and aroma of the cacao beans, undistracted by texture or sugar—which enhances desirable flavor and tames off-flavors. Each company has a specific liquor-tasting protocol. When a taster is tasting five or six liquors, it is standard practice to include a West African sample as a basic, neutral flavor reference. The lights of the tasting area are red to mask differences in color, forcing the tasters to focus on flavor.

Once the beans are accepted by the manufacturer and a master recipe for a particular chocolate has been formulated, the cacao beans are ready to be processed into chocolate.

For decades, cacao researchers were mostly concerned with selecting cacao specimens that were resistant to disease. In the last few years, however, their basic training has also begun to include an education in the sensory qualities of chocolate. Darin Sukha, a researcher at Trinidad's Cocoa Research Unit, melts cacao liquor prepared from several cacao genotypes for a comparative tasting. The primary goal of the test is to ascertain the relationship between flavor and genotype and to determine how flavor is affected by the post-harvest treatment of cacao (i.e., pod storage, fermentation, and drying).

# On to the Factory:
## Chocolate Achieved

Most chocolate manufacturers carry out more or less the same procedures in the same sequence, but the variations among the different cacaos brought by individual firms don't simply disappear at the factory gates. They dictate how the beans will be handled at certain stages. They are also responsible for the wide range of flavors and nuances clearly tasted in the finished chocolates.

When the beans arrive at the manufacturer, they are first run through a machine to remove foreign objects such as jute fibers, stones, or sticks as well as bits of loose hull or cacao placenta. They are then delivered to giant roasters. The roasting temperature and time depend on the type of bean and the desired effect. Fine, aromatic flavor beans are roasted for twenty to thirty minutes at temperatures between 220° and 240°F, changing the interior color to a richer brown. In general,

overroasting is a disservice to high-quality *criollo* cacao. *Forastero* cacao would ordinarily be roasted for a longer time.

The beans are now brittle, somewhat contracted, and easier to detach from the hulls. From the roaster, they go to a machine that crushes them just enough to winnow the hulls, or officially "shells," from the broken fragments of beans, or "nibs." The shells, which contain the bitter alkaloid theobromine, at one time were sold to make a cheap cocoa or coffee substitute (sometimes called "miserables" in Ireland); now they furnish theobromine for medical purposes and are sold as mulch for gardens. In Michoacán, Mexico, the roasted shells are further toasted, ground with aniseeds, and added to thick *atoles*. The nibs, just starting to be available for retail purchase, are prized as a new and valuable ingredient by discerning chefs and home cooks, but still nearly all go into commercial chocolate and cocoa processing.

The nibs are next crushed in high-speed mills and ground to a heavy mixture called

El Rey's state-of-the-art chocolate factory in Barquisimeto, Venezuela. To the far left, a Buhler five-roll refiner and a row of Frisse conches.

"cacao liquor" or "cocoa liquor," which is composed of cacao butter and cacao solids (mostly protein and starch). Despite the name "liquor," it is not alcoholic and would ordinarily be solid at room temperature. The brown gritty mass is further refined to break down the size of the particles. At this point, the liquor is ready to make chocolate. However, since most companies need a supply of cacao butter and cocoa powder, some of the liquor is diverted to hydraulic presses where the solids and butter are separated under pressures of more than six thousand pounds per square inch. Most large manufacturers also subject the cacao butter to a deodorizing process. This ensures that it will have a less emphatic effect when added later to chocolate made from miscellaneous lots of different cacao beans or when combined with milk and sugar to make the so-called white chocolate.

The butter content of the cacao liquor depends on the origin of the bean and fluctuates according to season and harvesting conditions. A Saint Lucia cacao may have barely 46.1 percent cacao butter by weight while the Brazilian Cruzeiro Sol tilts the scale with 61 percent. Venezuelan cacaos contain 51 to 60 percent butter. Normally chocolate manufacturers add additional cacao butter to some of their blends during conching to increase fluidity. The total percentage of cacao solids and butter used in a chocolate is called cacao "content." The higher the cacao content, the stronger the flavor, the lower the sugar. Discerning consumers should expect disclosure of this important information, for these percentages do have a bearing on the way chocolate behaves in many preparations—from a simple chocolate drink to an elegant ganache.

It is at this point that crucial ingredients like vanilla, sugar, and often some lecithin are mixed with the cacao liquor according to the manufacturer's formulation. For milk choco-

## CACAO BUTTER

Cacao butter is one of the most chemically intricate and challenging fats in nature. Like other fats, it consists mostly of triglycerides or compounds formed when three fatty acid molecules hook onto a glycerol molecule. The intricate part is that the three fatty acids on the resulting triglyceride molecule are almost always different kinds and would become solid or liquid at three slightly different temperatures. This is why the sensation of chocolate literally melting in your mouth is so unlike anything else. It is also the reason that people can have so much trouble working with melted chocolate.

late, powdered milk is added at the same time. The mass emerges from the mixer as sticky, gritty blobs of dark chocolate paste. A conveyor belt takes the paste to the refining machine where it is passed between gigantic steel rollers (set at varying widths) to reduce the particle size to between fourteen and twenty microns (about .0005 to .0007 inch). What comes out of the refiner is unrecognizable as chocolate, a light terra-cotta powderlike substance dusting the conveyor belt.

Finally the chocolate is conveyed into the conche, a more powerful and precise descendant of the one invented by Rodolphe Lindt more than a century ago. Today the purpose of the conche is not so much to break down the cacao particles (which has already been done by other machines) but to knead and agitate the cacao mass until it undergoes some not-fully-understood chemical changes that seem

to mellow, ripen, and round both flavor and texture. Some manufacturers conche only briefly, for four to five hours. The makers of premium chocolates have traditionally conched for about seventy-two hours or longer, though the time can be cut dramatically with the most efficient new conches. During conching, most manufacturers also adjust the fat content by adding some of the previously separated cacao butter and all or an additional percentage of the emulsifier lecithin, to give a more unctuous, satiny final result.

ABOVE: This anonymous print, which originally appeared in the German magazine *Die Gartenlaube,* shows women molding chocolate in a turn-of-the-century factory.

---

LEFT: Sticky blobs of dark chocolate paste emerge from the mixer. RIGHT: After being refined, the chocolate takes a powder-like form.

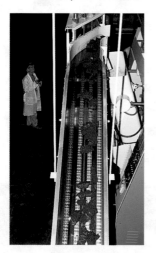 

THE NEW TASTE OF CHOCOLATE

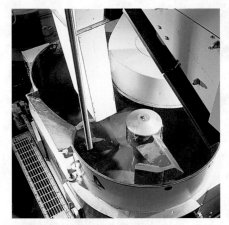

TOP, LEFT: A powerful conche heats and kneads milk chocolate to its final texture, flavor, and viscosity. TOP, RIGHT: Tempered chocolate is poured into plastic molds, which are then passed over a vibrating conveyor belt to settle the chocolate evenly in the mold and to expel air bubbles before cooling.

BOTTOM, LEFT AND RIGHT: Workers wrap chocolate bars manually for one of El Rey's domestic product lines.

The mass is sampled at intervals, and when deemed sufficiently conched, it is piped into large storage tanks that keep it warm. When the manufacturer is ready, the chocolate mass is piped into a tempering machine to realign the cacao butter crystals, just as a chef or home cook does it in the kitchen. The tempered chocolate is then poured into molds the size of the finished bar and passed over a conveyor belt that vibrates quickly to expel air bubbles. The molds pass through a cooling tunnel from which the solid, shiny chocolate goes to the wrapping station. The speed of the conveyor belt and the temperature of the tunnel are critical variables. At many factories, the wrapping is done by machine. In others, or for certain lines of chocolate, workers unmold and manually wrap each bar.

That would be the end of the perilous journey of our cacao, except that the chocolate still has to get to the store and the consumer. If it is mishandled en route, it can lose temper, absorb obnoxious odors, or become discolored by a surface "bloom."

## The Mysterious Subtleties of Chocolate Flavor

The lingering fruitiness you detect in a piece of chocolate from one maker, the subtle hint of bitter almonds in another, even such notes as the tealike flavor or odd, faint accent of Swiss cheese or some other dairy product in some dark chocolates are not refinements created at the factory. They come from the latent genetic "messages" inherent in the cacao itself, which are "translated" into detectable characteristics during fermentation. The process mysteriously unleashes the so-called chocolate-flavor precursors in the cacao bean.

But the creation of flavor and aroma does not end with fermentation. When the cacao is spread out to dry, the combined heat of the sun and the chemical reactions going on within the beans can raise the temperature of the mass to as much as 120°F, imparting  the sort of warm, subtle suavity that you find in some roasted foods like potatoes.

When it comes to drying, there may be other local differences. Every cacao-growing area of the world must plant for its own climatic conditions. Regions that harvest a lot of their cacao during the rainy season or with cloudy weather—including much of Brazil, Southeast Asia, parts of West Africa, and the Indian Ocean—must use artificial drying methods to decrease the moisture content.

None of these is as effective as sun-drying. Much cacao is dried over smoky wood fires on the Indonesian island of Java, giving it a flavor that reminds most people of smoked ham and me (the Latin cook) of chorizo-type sausage. This is all the more curious because the Java stock has a lot of *criollo* ancestry and would otherwise have classic *criollo* flavor. In the Bahia region of Brazil, people use gas-fired dryers that can also impart undesirable flavors. Even without such flaws, a common problem with any sort of mechanical drying is that it may not reproduce the smooth sequence of enzymatic and other changes achieved by several days in the sun. The resulting chocolate flavor can be sour, harsh, or flat.

During roasting, cacao gains sweetness and a hint of caramel together with floral and earthy notes. Flavors are rounded off when the cacao mass is combined with sugar and vanilla during mixing, and when the mass is reduced in particle size by passing through the refiner. More flavor develops when the cacao mass is conched and heated in the conching machines. While the heated mass achieves that smooth texture we associate with fine-quality chocolate, it also expels volatile acids that contribute to acidity. There is a delicate balance between reducing excess acidity and eliminating the seductive fruitiness that a small amount of acid can contribute to some chocolates.

## Cacao: Flavor Beans and Bulk Beans

Chocolate manufacturers have a world of cacao beans at their disposal. Their choices are as varied and exciting as the colors on a painter's palette—large dabs of basic black and white with a dozen smaller dashes of color, some pure and radiant like the cobalt blue and saturated red of a medieval stained glass window. The gemlike primary colors of this palette are the finest cacaos in the world—the precious and glistening remnants of true *criollos* that account for less than 1 percent of world production: the perfumed Chuao, the nutty *porcelana,* the citrusy and delicate Java. Secondary and tertiary colors, the ones resulting from mixing, are the flavorful *trinitarios* with their hybrid vigor and the good bones of their *criollo* parents.

Of all *trinitarios,* the ones from Trinidad, their reputed birthplace, are the most coveted. They combine the strength of the *forastero* and its resistance to disease with the flavor and aroma of the more fragile *criollo. Trinitarios* are classified as fine flavor beans and sell way above the international market price for cacao, though production has been on a steady decline in recent years, primarily because of severe labor shortages.

In Trinidad there are two basic grades of beans: plantation grade, which is the finest, with plump, perfect beans, and estate grade, with beans of varying sizes and some imperfections allowed. In Trinidad, beans are polished after drying, which greatly improves their appearance, and as some Trinitarians claim, helps to protect the beans from insect infestation. Today polishing is done by machine, but not so long ago it was done "by foot." East Indian workers danced on the cacao, rubbing the beans between their feet to polish them.

Also a part of this first family of cacao, though of different progeny, is the now-rare Arriba from Ecuador, which is often (not without controversy) classified as a *forastero.* The trade classifies these beans as "fine cacao" or "flavor beans," and they account for less than 5 percent of the world's estimated 2,500,000 metric tons of cacao produced yearly.

Flavor beans dazzle with their complexity. The very best among them, the ones that have been treated wiscly, offer an exhilarating ride for the taste buds—not one but many notes of flavor explode in the mouth while the essence of pure deep chocolate lingers softly for a long time.

Trinidad plantation grade beans

Trinidad estate grade beans

# Venezuela

**SUR DEL LAGO CLASIFICADO**
Zulia State
*Criollo*

**CRIOLLO ANDINO**
Venezuelan Andes (Mérida State)
*Criollo*

**CASERIO VEGA DEL PUENTE**
Barinitas, Barinas State
*Forastero*

**OCUMARE 67 X IMC 67**
Finca San Joaquin, Barinas State
*Trinitario with a strong criollo germplasm*

**TRINCHERAS**
Carabobo State
*Trinitario*

**CUYAGUA**
Cuyagua, Aragua State
*Criollo and trinitario blend*

**OCUMARE DE LA COSTA**
Ocumare de la Costa, Aragua State
*Criollo and trinitario blend*

THE NEW TASTE OF CHOCOLATE

# Venezuela

**CHORONÍ**
La Sabaneta, Aragua State
*Criollo and trinitario blend*

**CHUAO**
Aragua State
*Criollo and trinitario blend*

**CARENERO SUPERIOR**
Hacienda La Concepción, Miranda State
*Trinitario*

**GUARIBE (GUARIMÍ MOUNTAIN)**
Guárico and Miranda States
*Trinitario*

**RÍO CARIBE (unfermented)**
Yaguaraparo, Paria Peninsula (Sucre State)
*Trinitario*

**RÍO CARIBE (fermented)**
Finca Francescchi, Paria Peninsula (Sucre State)
*Trinitario*

**ARRIBA, ECUADOR**
*Forastero*

**TABASCO, MEXICO (UNFERMENTED)**
*Forastero*

**GUAYAQUIL, ECUADOR**
*Forastero*

**GRENADA**
*Trinitario*

**BAHIA, BRAZIL**
*Forastero*

**SAN JUAN ESTATE, TRINIDAD**
*Trinitario*

*Africa*　　　　*Indian Ocean*

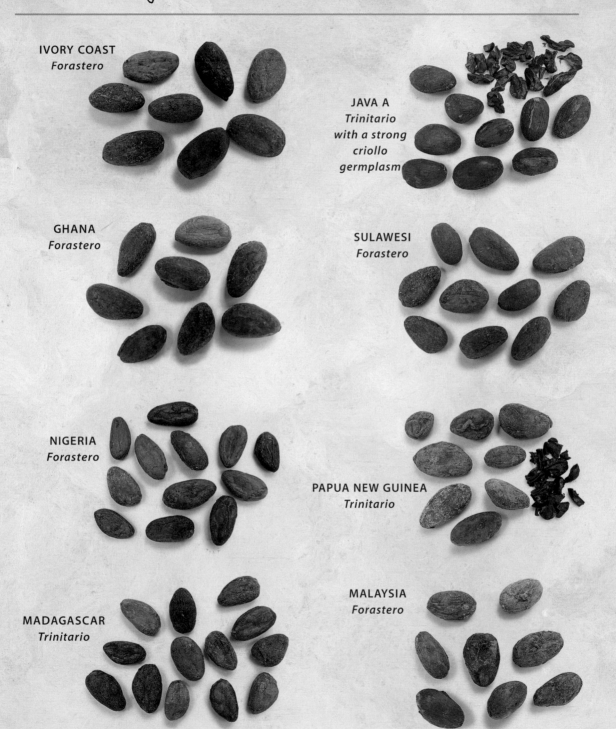

**IVORY COAST**
*Forastero*

**JAVA A**
*Trinitario
with a strong
criollo
germplasm*

**GHANA**
*Forastero*

**SULAWESI**
*Forastero*

**NIGERIA**
*Forastero*

**PAPUA NEW GUINEA**
*Trinitario*

**MADAGASCAR**
*Trinitario*

**MALAYSIA**
*Forastero*

The essential blacks and whites are "bulk" cacao beans, the reliable *forasteros* that give necessary body or bulk to many chocolate blends. Ideally, they provide a solid core of satisfactory—or better—chocolate flavor. Some *forasteros,* however, are poorly fermented and miserably acrid.

The bulk beans account for more than 90 percent of the world's cacao production. West Africa ranks first in world production, with the Ivory Coast taking the lead over Ghana, which not long ago was the continent's premier producer. Indonesia does not lag far behind the Ivory Coast, having surpassed Malaysia in recent years. One of the largest producers of bulk cacao in Indonesia is Sulawesi.

The largest cacao producer in Latin America, Brazil is still an important player. But since the 1950s, production has been on the decline, as witches' broom and black pod rot have decimated the country's most productive regions. In the late 1990s, Brazil began to import cacao from West Africa to satisfy internal demand for chocolate. A surprisingly large Latin producer is the Dominican Republic, with production fluctuating between 30,000 to 43,000 metric tons at the end of the twentieth century. Cacao has been commercially grown on Hispaniola (the large Caribbean island now shared by Haiti and the Dominican Republic) with varying degrees of success since the seventeenth century. Though the island's cacao population is a mixed batch of Lower Amazon *forasteros* (similar to the *matina* of Costa Rica and the *ceylan* of Tabasco), *trinitarios,* and even some *criollos* from Venezuela, the bulk of the crop is represented by *forasteros.* Dominican cacao is known to the trade by the generic name of Sánchez, after the port from which it was traditionally shipped. In recent years, its former

### DANCING THE CACAO

In this late nineteenth century photograph, East Indian workers in Trinidad "dance" over a patch of cacao beans drying in the sun to give the beans a desirable sheen. Nowadays, this process is done by machines. Workers pour the dried beans into a large metal pan fitted with a removable perforated wooden floor and rotating wooden paddles that keep the beans from touching the metal. The beans are wetted slightly and then stirred by the rotating paddles. Electric or gasoline-generated blowers blow cool air from below. When the polishing is over, the beans are dried with hot air. The friction generated by this process gives premium Trinidad beans their characteristic clean, appealing shine.

reputation as an astringent, bitter, unfermented cacao has been improved by more attentive post-harvest treatment.

There are amazing flavor variations among bulk beans. Nigerian *forasteros* are robust with strong roasted-coffee notes. When Bahia beans are well fermented and sun-dried, they have more of an even-keeled flavor; but when they are machine-dried, their acidity varies wildly, from the quirky squeeze of fresh lime in a *caipirinha* to an overdose of vinegar in your salad. When Dominican Sánchez beans are unfermented, they are nondescript and smell like burnt rubber. Well-fermented, they can compare with some of the reliable Ivory Coast beans.

Ghana—where the government enforces very stringent standards of quality—produces an especially sought-after bulk cacao of very reliable quality, with a slightly nutty flavor and a suggestion of roast coffee. The beans come mostly from Lower Amazon *forasteros*—genetically related to the Brazilian *"comum"*—which have been fully fermented and sun-dried on mats. They deliver clean, good chocolate flavor with no bangs or fanfare. They come with no surprises, lasting just long enough in your mouth to let you know you are eating chocolate and leaving you with neither disappointment nor exhilaration. They are favored by many manufacturers because they are also neutral in acidity; thus cacao liquor made from Ghana beans is often used in sensory evaluation testing as a standard of reference for other liquors.

But in every family there are scoundrels. For them, the trade has an unflattering name: "dogs and cats." These are either cacao beans that have some undesirable characteristic such as extreme acidity, or poor grades of better cacaos that have been rejected for some flaw in processing, such as overfermentation or moldiness. These cacaos are used to provide bulk in some inferior brands of chocolate or are processed into cocoa powder and cacao butter.

Heaps of lumpy, moldy overfermented cacao beans are laid out to dry. They will be sold at a fraction of the price of premium-quality beans and used to manufacture cacao butter.

## CACAO BEAN FASHION

Since cacao was first exported to Europe, different regional cacaos have succeeded each other at intervals in general favor or disfavor. By the nineteenth century, the once-prized cacao of Mexico had been so debased that knowledgeable consumers (even in Mexico) often passed it by for the Venezuelan Caracas, Maracaibo, and Puerto Cabello, and the Colombian Magdalena. In the esteemed Venezuelan producing area of Paria Peninsula, the *trinitario* cacao formerly called "Carúpano" (for the port city from which it is still shipped) wore out its welcome when formerly high standards of care declined. The cacao had to be rebaptized "Río Caribe"

(the name of another coastal town in Paria) to be accepted when its quality improved. This shows how intensely people identified particular regional origins with definite characteristics. One reason is that the genetic base of cacao used to be less promiscuously mingled; experts tasting cacao beans or chocolate recognized a spectrum of flavors that pointed to origins.

In place of the coveted Caracas, Venezuela now exports a distinct type called "Carenero," which comes from the fertile and humid region of Barlovento, northeast of Caracas. (The name Carenero comes from the small port from which the cacao used to be shipped to La Guaira in colonial times.) The plantations of this area grow a mixed bunch of *trinitarios* and *forasteros*, but the best growers propagate their cacao by selecting the ones with stronger *criollo* germplasm. Select, well-fermented beans from Barlovento are sold as "Carenero Superior" and are prized by manufacturers for their complex lingering chocolate flavor and aroma, spiciness, and characteristic fruitiness. The beans can be recognized immediately for their unique *goût de terroir*. The number of cacaos that retain such a distinctive character has shrunk drastically.

The premium light-colored Java beans (classified as Java A) are getting so expensive and hard to find that manufacturers are switching allegiance to the once-obscure cacao of Madagascar, which has a similar color and a subtle citrus acidity. Plump hybrids from Ecuador are penetrating the market, though the coveted floral Arriba, long a favorite of many American manufacturers, is now a rarity.

Heirloom beans from particular regions and single plantations represent a minute frac-

### THAT WAS THEN, THIS IS NOW

The eighty-year-old Silvio Crespo, longtime technical director at Wilbur Chocolate Company in Lititz, Pennsylvania, once told me that he could tell which beans were roasting from the parking lot, so distinct was their aroma. That's no longer possible, he claims:

> In the "good old days," we were able to pinpoint cacao beans by areas, variety, and/or countries such as Maracaibo, Caracas, Puerto Cabello, Arriba, Accra, etc. Today we call them Venezuelan, Ecuadorian, African, etc. with exception of the Far Eastern ones, which we still call Java, Samoan, Malaysian, etc. Before long, most of the cacao beans will be grown from hybrids, clones, and God only knows what other ways—mainly, to reach large yield productions, and to develop a variety that resists the many enemies of the cacao plantations.... What will happen to flavor cacao beans then?

THE NEW TASTE OF CHOCOLATE

tion of the cacao bean trade. Their survival lies in the hands of fine manufacturers and discerning consumers.

## The New Taste of Chocolate

The face of chocolate has changed fantastically in the last five to ten years, and shoppers now find themselves confronted with some bewildering choices between blended chocolates and a newer breed of "exclusive-derivation" chocolates.

The word "blended" is one recurrent source of misunderstanding. What it means is that the cacao beans are of different varieties and/or geographical origins. Do not assume that the result is necessarily an anonymous, homogenized hodgepodge. The practice of blending is very old, indeed pre-Columbian. From the start it was founded on a recognition that the right combinations of different cacaos have a kind of synergy, a total effect greater than the sum of the parts. But to achieve the full potential the maker must treat each variety with regard to its special needs (for example, optimal roasting temperature). This was part of the skill possessed by the older European artisanal chocolate makers.

### A RECIPE FOR CHOCOLATE

Cookbooks or culinary encyclopedias used to give suggested custom blends of beans like this one from *Nuevo Cocinero Americano en Forma de Diccionario,* published in Mexico in 1873:

| | |
|---|---|
| Soconusco | 2 pounds |
| Maracaybo | 2 pounds |
| Caracas | 2 pounds |

Sugar, 4 to 6 pounds allowing for some preferring it sweeter than others, and an equal number of ounces of cinnamon, making allowance for the irritability of people's stomachs or for each person's taste. Tabasco [cacao] can also be used in place of Maracaybo, but chocolate made with it has less body.

The anonymous contributor also adds optional ingredients like ground biscuit and almonds, but remarks that too much of them makes the chocolate stop being chocolate. Formulas like this show how integral the idea of blending has been to the whole enjoyment of chocolate through the years.

364     *Of Drinkables.*

## CHAP. VIII.

### *Of* CHOCOLATE.

YOU are to chuse that which is new made, heavy enough, hard and dry, of a brown reddish Colour, good Smell, and pleasant Taste.

Chocolate is nourishing enough: It is strengthning, restorative, and apt to repair decay'd Strength, and make People strong: It helps Digestion, allays the sharp Humours that fall upon the Lungs: It keeps down the Fumes of Wine, promotes Venery, and resists the Malignity of the Humours.

When Chocolate is taken to Excess, or that you use a great many sharp and pungent Drugs in the making of it, it heats much, and hinders several People from sleep.

The Cocoa, which is the principal Ingredient for making Chocolate, as we shall observe by and by, contains much Oil and essential Salt; as for the other Drugs which are mixt with it, they are all full of exalted Oil and volatile Salt.

Chocolate agrees, especially in cold Weather, with old People, with cold and phlegmatic Persons, and with those that cannot easily digest their Food, because of the Weakness and Nicety of their Stomachs; but young People of a hot and bilious Constitution, whose Humours are already too much in stitution, ought to abstain from it, or use it very Motioately.

From *A Treatise of All Sorts of Foods* by M. L. Lemery, 1745

When the corporate giants came on the scene, they adapted the time-honored tradition of blending to the pursuit of profit more than flavor. But do not imagine that Cadbury, Nestle, and Hershey were blind to the distinctions between good and bad cacaos. They never lost sight of a complex calculus between price and quality, enabling them to give cheap, commonplace *forasteros* a flavor boost from carefully judged smaller admixtures of better beans.

Depending on the sensory profile they are after, manufacturers might start with a large percentage of a good reliable *forastero,* frequently from West Africa. Then they would blend in some of the more popular flavor beans (often suave Venezuelan *criollos* with some gutsier, fruitier *trinitarios*). The finishing touch might be a small dash of some rare, uniquely scented cacao (the endangered Ecuadorian Arriba or the elite *criollos,* such as *porcelana* or true Chuao). The sensory profile might also include a certain desired appearance, for example, using Java beans to provide a pale color in milk chocolate.

## SORTING OUT "EXCLUSIVE-DERIVATION" CHOCOLATES

When a new, ambitious generation of bold chocolatiers came along in the 1990s, some took the blending route and others came out with chocolates that identified the origin of the cacao beans or the name of an estate on the label. "Single-variety," "single-origin" *(origen único),* "*grand cru,*" "pure origin," and even "estate-grown" have become the buzz words in chocolate making today. For the sake of convenience I refer to this cluster of offerings as "exclusive-derivation chocolates." There are

parallels between wine making and chocolate making in this respect, though we should remember that wine grapes and cacao are analogous only up to a point.

Chocolate made only from cacao grown in one region (single-origin), or even a single plantation (estate-grown), will almost invariably turn out to be a blend of botanical varieties, for very few modern plantations grow one cacao strain alone, and any growing region or country is bound to have various hybrids. A bag of Grenada beans, for example, might contain beans from Upper Amazon *forasteros* such as Scavina 6 or IMC 67 (Iquitos Mixed Calabacillo), *trinitarios* like ICS 1 (Imperial College Selection 1 from Trinidad), and Grenada Select Hybrids from the island's original *criollo* population. And theoretically— though this is a less likely scenario—you could call a chocolate "single-variety" as long as it contained only one specific cacao variety, no matter whether the cacao came from one region or three different countries. What distinguishes one natural blend from the other is a matter of the local soil and environment bringing out inherent genetic characteristics, and the way in which particular styles of drying and fermentation have distinct effects on overall flavor and aroma.

The advantage of the exclusive-derivation approach, when practiced by knowledgeable chocolatiers, is that the individual nuances of a particular bean will register very clearly on the palate. Sometimes you can almost get a cacao education at a single bite—a rare pleasure that few chocolate lovers have had the chance to experience until very recently.

LEFT AND BELOW: Chocovic, the modern reincarnation of Xocolat Arumi, a nineteenth-century Catalan chocolate factory, is proud of its "origen único" (single origin) line of chocolates made exclusively with cacao beans from Guayaquil (Ecuador), the island of Grenada, and Barlovento (Venezuela).

ABOVE: In 1998, Valrhona added a new vintage estate chocolate to its roster of "grand crus." Chocolat Noir de Domaine Gran Couva is manufactured with *trinitario* beans from Philippe Agostini's San Juan Estate, an old Corsican plantation near the town of Gran Couva.

The single-origin approach works beautifully when the beans in question are exceptionally good and noble and have had good post-harvest treatment, giving them a well-rounded, complex flavor and aroma. Chocolates El Rey, the Venezuelan chocolate manufacturer and grower that was first in identifying the source of its beans in 1994, buys only fully fermented Carenero Superior beans from Barlovento. The result is a line of single-origin chocolates, ranging from a seductive milk chocolate with 41 percent cacao content (Caoba) to a robust extra bitter dark chocolate with 70 percent cacao content (Gran Samán),

which have lately been joined by chocolates that contain higher contents of cacao butter added to the dark chocolate formulas. Though made with the same regional blend of Carenero Superior beans, the varying amounts of sugar and cacao butter in the formulas of the different chocolates play to their distinct notes of fruit, nut, and spice in different keys.

The same is true of single-estate chocolates that blend good-quality, expertly fermented *criollos* and *trinitarios* raised on one farm, such as El Rey's San Joaquín and Valrhona's Chocolat Noir de Domaine Gran Couva (64 percent cacao content). The latter is made with polished "Plantation Grade" *trini-tario* beans from San Juan Estate, an old colonial plantation in Trinidad.

But shoppers new to the intricacies of today's chocolate lingo may not understand one loophole in exclusive-derivation terms: If the beans are terrible to begin with, no claim about variety, origin, or *cru* will ever raise the resulting chocolate above the level of the very worst mass-produced blend. Another surprise for novices may be that distinguished *criollo* or *trinitario* strains aren't the only source of exclu-sive-derivation chocolates. There are some *forastero* cacaos that (when well handled) can yield pleasing chocolate. Some large companies like Callebaut traditionally have gone this route, and other makers are doing it today. The Swiss-owned Barry Callebaut (the offspring of a merger between the Belgian giant Callebaut and France's Cacao Barry) recently launched a line of exclusive-derivation chocolates using *forasteros* carefully screened for the purpose— from the Dominican Republic, Ecuador, and Indonesia.

El Rey's San Joaquín Estate "Grand Cru" is Venezuela's first entry in the growing international ranks of estate-grown chocolate. The chocolate is fruity with a pronounced peach flavor, subtle citrus notes, a floral bouquet, and a distinctive earthy accent that calls for the Spanish phrase *sabor a bosque* ("flavor of the woods").

---

Launched in 1999, the first entry in Cacao Barry's Origine Rare line is a dark couverture (70% cacao content) manufactured with Cuban beans from the Baracoa region in northeastern Cuba. Due to trade restrictions, this chocolate is not available in the United States. Pleasantly smoky with a subtle tobacco undertone and a citrusy edge, this chocolate is produced in small batches since Cuba's cacao production is limited and mostly destined to national consumption and the production of cacao butter for international markets.

THE NEW TASTE OF CHOCOLATE

## EXCLUSIVE-DERIVATION OR BLENDED: WHICH IS BETTER?

People new to the appreciation of chocolate often ask which is better, the exclusive-derivation or the blended approach. Both options have equal validity. But as one who thinks the unexamined chocolate is not worth eating, I'd say that the piece of information missing here is the cacao's origin (or origins). This should be on every package from supermarket candy wrappers to boxes of *luxe* truffles.

Today's boutique chocolatiers have no reason to follow the example of old-style corporate giants who treat their blending formulas as state secrets, and every reason to tell information-hungry aficionados the exact origin and variety of all the cacao in their chocolate. A common argument against disclosure is the manufacturer's need to replace some cacaos from time to time in their blends. Yet this should be a part of the informational literature handed out to consumers.

The labeling issue has another dimension related to the disturbing shifts and disappearances that I've described taking place in the global roster of cacao varieties. Truly excellent cacaos currently represent less than 2 percent of the international cacao bean trade, while a few mediocre cultivars increase their comparative share by leaps and bounds. Who will have any incentive to carry on the demanding task of growing yesterday's rare and exquisite cacaos if today's industry fails to demand fine

**BAY AREA BOUTIQUE BLENDS**

In spring 2000, the San Francisco Bay Area's Guittard Chocolates unveiled a new line of couvertures. These boutique blends feature a high cacao content and a large percentage of heirloom Venezuelan beans deftly combined with premium beans, such as the aromatic Ecuadorian Arriba. Through such innovations, Gary Guittard pushed his company to the forefront of the new chocolate revolution. These new offerings were inspired by the recipes and labels created in the nineteenth century by Étienne Guittard, the company's founder and Gary Guittard's French-born grandfather—another example of how the past is shaping the new taste of chocolate.

flavor beans, pay premium prices for them, and make their names well known to adventurous food lovers? When information about provenance routinely appears on labels, the friends of fine chocolate may be able to strike a few blows for heirloom cacao from particular regions or even particular farms.

The many cacao varieties are a vivid and fascinating array of botanical "personalities." The place to start recognizing the nuts and bolts of the finely tuned construction that you experience as flavor compositions from the likes of Bernachon, El Rey, Guittard, Scharffen Berger, Omanhene, and Valrhona is in the nature of individual cacaos.

ABOVE: At the end of 1994 the manufacturer El Rey launched its Carenero Superior line, the first chocolate that included labeling information about the origin of the beans to reach the American market. The original Carenero line featured three distinctive chocolates, to which a fourth product (a white chocolate) was added in 1997. The line now includes three other high cacao–content chocolates.

LEFT: Manufactured in Ghana from 100 percent Ghanaian beans, Omanhene is an exclusive-derivation dark milk chocolate made with good-quality bulk beans.

THE NEW TASTE OF CHOCOLATE

Scharffen Berger chocolate bars with a variety of cacao contents

## CUSTOM-BLEND CHOCOLATE

Notable achievements of the blending approach are chocolates from small makers such as the famous chocolatier Maurice Bernachon in Lyon. Together with his son Jean Jacques, Bernachon makes his own chocolate blend using as many as thirteen types of cacao, mostly "flavor" beans from South America, including Chuao from Venezuela, which he regards as the world's best.

In small factories several high-quality beans can be independently roasted and blended in small batches to achieve a high level of quality. This is what Robert Steinberg—who once trained with Bernachon—and John Scharffenberger do at their San Francisco factory, using vintage equipment like an old German mélangeur with gigantic granite rollers to crush the cacao nibs, the sugar, and whole vanilla beans. Their emphasis is on high flavor. Their formula is composed of 50 percent Venezuelan flavor beans, such as Carenero Superior from Barlovento and Sur del Lago Clasificado from the Lake Maracaibo area, as well as *trinitarios* from Trinidad, Madagascar, Java, and occasionally Papua New Guinea. They also use *forasteros* like the reliable Ghana, and occasionally the more acid Bahia—not as bulk beans to add body to the chocolate but as flavor notes in a complex synthesis of elements. What you taste in their rich chocolate (70 percent cacao content)—marvelous fruit with hints of citrus and cherries, mild astringency, subtle bitter almond undertaste, and long chocolate finish—is the result of blending choices.

# Identifying Cacao

No food plant is more difficult to arrange in logical classifications than cacao. It does not have a large genome (the diploid chromosome number is only twenty), but when we start trying to apply such different criteria as the outward appearance of the pod, the color and shape of the beans, and the flavor characteristics passed on from generation to generation, we quickly find ourselves in layer upon layer of confusion.

With some tree fruits, there may be some genetic puzzles, but it is fairly clear how most of the modern cultivars are related to parents. Cacao is another case. Until the age of DNA analysis, the ancestries of important strains and their offshoots have been mostly indecipherable, and the ways in which a cacao tree's complement of genes find expression defy simple description. The language of breeders and agronomists is the only existing vehicle for identifying the major cultivars responsible for the chocolate we eat.

## Morphological Types

Morphology is the study of structure and form in living organisms. It gives us a convenient way to classify cacaos by external characteristics. For a long time there were no other tools for distinguishing one kind from another. The various names that sprang up to describe cacao varieties during the colonial period have been superseded by others for purposes of genetic identification, but they are still useful as general descriptors.

ABOVE: Frances Bekele, an expert in cacao morphology. She is currently working on a classification project for the Cocoa Research Unit in Trinidad.

OPPOSITE: Cacao pods display a diversity of sizes, shapes, textures, and colors.

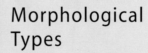

*Amelonado.* Pods have a melonlike shape that has been described as resembling a cantaloupe crossed with a football, with thick, usually smooth skins and occasionally some wartiness. The pod has shallow ridges and furrows and the tip is rounded rather than pointed. At most, it shows a faint hint of a bottleneck.

*Calabacillo.* Reflecting its name, this cacao has the shape of a small pumpkin (*calabaza* is the Spanish name for pumpkin). It is round or oval, with thick and very smooth skin. It has almost no ridges or furrows, and no suggestion of tip or bottleneck. Usually it is on the small side. Unlike most cacaos, it has a characteristic color: grass green changing to a beautiful deep yellow as it matures.

*Angoleta.* Pods are long and ridged but less warty and furrowed than *cundeamor,* with wide shoulders and little or no bottleneck. The tip is usually somewhat pointed but not curved.

*Cundeamor.* The name *cundeamor* (also spelled *cundiamor*) originally referred to a somewhat similar-looking fruit that is in the same genus as the Chinese bitter melon. These cacaos have long, warty, deeply ridged and furrowed pods, with either a pronounced bottleneck or a suggestion of one at the stem end and a pointed tip ("apex") that is curved in some varieties. The most exaggerated example of the *cundeamor* type is *pentagona* (*Theobroma cacao* var. *pentagona,* see page 94).

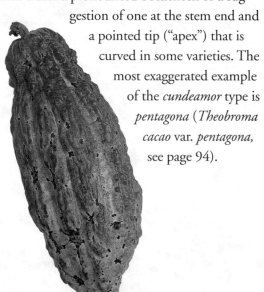

THE NEW TASTE OF CHOCOLATE

# The Many Faces of Cacao

Let's take a look at some important cacao cultivars. Some are old cacaos whose origin is surrounded with some mystery; others are genebank creations engineered by scientists. We are not yet at the point of knowing exactly how the "information" locked within the genes of a cacao plant translates into everything we see in the actual plant. Time and again we find ourselves explaining that Cacao A must have arisen by interbreeding with distant cousin Cacao B or C, leading to a vast tangle of names. But for the sake of convenience, I shall follow the currently accepted classification of three main races that originated in different areas of South America: *criollo, forastero,* and *trinitario.*

What might seem peculiar is that some of the cacaos pictured in this identification section don't always find their names printed on a bag of beans. Cacao beans are normally sold under the name of the country or—more rarely now—the region of origin or port of shipment. Though Ghana cacao is a *forastero* cacao mostly of the *amelonado* type, you will never see it sold as such in the international market. Indiscriminate hybridization has also contributed to muddled distinctions between different strains. The beans produced on a single plantation or in a particular region might literally be a mixed bag of several cultivars that will never receive individual credit. But here you'll get to see some important varieties with their corresponding beans. I have used specimens provided by scientists and progressive growers from some of the world's finest plantations and genebanks.

## A WRINKLE IN CLASSIFICATION

Recent collection expeditions in French Guiana have opened another field of inquiry—the area's wild cacao, though shaped like an *amelonado,* has little in common genetically with either Upper or Lower Amazon *forasteros.* This has created yet another wrinkle within the present system of classification. Already, Philip Lachanaud, a French scientist at Centre de Cooperátion Internationale en Recherche Agronomique pour le Développement (CIRAD), is proposing a new system of classification with four major groups: *criollos* from Central America, Colombia, and Venezuela; Amazons, including Upper Amazon *forasteros;* Guayanan, embracing the whole of the Guiana's plateau, which is shared by Venezuela, Surinam, French Guiana, and Brazil; and Ecuadorian *Nacional* or Arriba. This system has been presented as a working hypothesis that needs further refinement and field research.

# Criollos

## WESTERN VENEZUELAN CRIOLLOS

If there is one place where we are likely to find pure *criollos,* it is in the western reaches of Venezuela wandering toward the Colombian border. Broadly speaking, there are two cacao environments here. One is the area called Sur del Lago: the humid, marshy lands south and west of Lake Maracaibo, once the source of the beautiful "Maracaibo" beans prized by connoisseurs. The other area lies farther westward and is the highest terrain on which cacao has established itself: the foothills of the Venezuelan Andes. The strains that grow here are collectively called Andean *criollos (criollos andinos).*

## PORCELANA: THE HOLY GRAIL OF PURE CRIOLLOS

It seems that the Spaniards found cultivated cacao in western Venezuela upon their arrival. An early sixteenth-century entry in Venezuela's national records describes thousands of cacao trees growing in rows south of Lake Maracaibo. This humid hothouse is home to the holy grail of pure *criollos,* the exquisite cacao called *porcelana.* It was probably synonymous with most of the old Maracaibo cacao, though it had such unique status that it actually shows up as the most expensive cacao in documents of the nineteenth-century Hamburg cacao exchange.

Scattered *porcelana* groves can still be found in the basin of the Escalante River, which drains into Lake Maracaibo. You can also find trees in mixed-variety plantations along with currently more popular cultivars, such as the *amelonado*-type cacao called *pajarito.* But all local cacao farming is under siege here as more and more farmers are cutting down cacao trees and starting to grow less demanding crops such as oranges or bananas, or to raise cattle.

Can this lovely cacao be saved? After visiting an experimental farm sponsored by the government of Zulia state and run by a team of state agronomists, I think the answer may be

LEFT AND OPPOSITE: Red *porcelana* pods
OPPOSITE, INSET: Detail from *Venezuela cum parte Australe Novae Andalusiae* by Henricus Hondius, 1642 (see page 25). The humid flatlands of Lake Maracaibo in Venezuela are the home of *porcelana,* the world's most coveted *criollo.*

THE NEW TASTE OF CHOCOLATE

yes. Estación Experimental Chama, located near the town of El Vigía, about twenty-five miles south of Lake Maracaibo, is a germplasm bank for pure *porcelana*. This seven-acre plantation is dedicated to the preservation and propagation of this variety, a vestige of commercial cacao's Golden Age.

The farm, set in the muggy and buggy green flats of Sur del Lago, has the look of a traditional plantation cordoned into tracts by irrigation ditches, the trees planted at generous (by modern standards) 3- by 3-meter intervals. Of course I have walked through many cacao groves, but this was a delicious experience in

A mixed batch of *porcelana* pods and other Sur del Lago cacaos—including some specimens of *pajarito*, an *amelonado* from nearby Colombia—are stored for five days before opening to improve flavor.

Red and green *porcelana* pods showing the characteristic white and light pick cotyledons and large plump beans of a true *criollo* (center). A homespun chocolate bar prepared with *porcelana* beans (top, left).

itself. The big shade trees were mamey sapotes *(Pouteria sapote)*—one of the most beloved of Latin American fruits. The fruits were ripe when I visited and the beige brown mameys squashed underfoot as I walked, tempting me to pick them up and munch on their salmon-colored flesh.

When you see *porcelana* cacao growing on the tree, you understand where the name came from. Some of the unripe pods are a translucent green enamel that makes you think of celadon ware or Chinese jade carvings. Some are as red as Snow White's apple, or dappled with a pinkish hue. When fully ripe, they may be orange-red or light yellow shot with green. What astonished me, and must also have completely amazed the first Spanish cacao entrepreneurs to set eyes on it, is that the fruit is completely smooth (when spared by insects), an anomaly among *criollos.* The shape can be nearly as oval as a typical *amelonado,* sometimes with a suggestion of a bottleneck or faint ridges, or it can be long and skinny, almost daggerlike. The giveaway to its identity is the conspicuous nipplelike tip.

Insects such as thrips had carved many pods with miniature moonscapes or huge pockmarks and meandering trails. These invaders can do much worse to the usually fragile *porcelana* variety. They can chew the thin-skinned pods badly enough to leave them easy prey for squirrels or deadly fungal diseases. But the trees of the Chama facility seemed healthy and had managed to escape moniliasis, the scourge of this humid region.

Transplanting shade tree seedlings at Estación Experimental Chama

This facility has no commercial output but supplies *porcelana* seedlings and clones grown in its large nursery to farmers interested in reviving the historic strain. On several occasions I was given laboratory samples of chocolate made with *porcelana* by a manufacturer testing the potential of different Venezuelan cacaos. While visiting Chama, the head agronomist gave me a large bar she had made of well-fermented *porcelana* beans in all their gritty, homespun glory, using a disposable aluminum container as a mold. If you were to sample it along with chocolates made with other Venezuelan cacaos, it would be the least acidic or fruity— you would find it as neutral and nutty as a buttery macadamia, with low levels of astringency and bitterness. This comes as a surprise to people who are expecting a crowded busload of flavors. What is striking about *porcelana* is its pure and powerful lingering chocolate flavor and aroma as well as its delicate notes of spice.

To my knowledge, there is no pure *porcelana* coming out of this region, but rather a mixed batch that combines other *trinitarios* and *porcelana* with Colombian *pajarito.* The blending is only half of the problem. Properly fermented and dried, this natural blend of cacao beans would yield a flavorful chocolate. But post-harvest practices in this very humid region are poor and lag behind other regions of Venezuela. It is not uncommon to detect musty, hay, and even jute bag off-flavors and smells in a good-looking sample of Sur del Lago Clasificado beans (the premium classification that has come to replace the old Maracaibo label).

I have seen in Chama *porcelana* beans of the highest quality, a pure white that instantly gives away their unmixed *criollo* ancestry. Here lies the proof that good *porcelana* plantations could still be viable today. Certainly the market exists among knowledgeable chocolatiers.

Venezuelan scientists examine a Guasare pod for signs of disease. Right to left: Gladys Ramos Carranza and Antonio Azócar, of the Campo Experimental San Juan de Lagunillas, and visiting scientists Humberto Reyes and Lilian Capriles de Reyes.

## GUASARE

Some years ago, people in the cacao business started hearing tales about a remarkably fine cacao showing up at market in small amounts. It came from the mountainous area of the Sierra de Perijá, close to the Colombian border. Where was it being grown? At last the specific source was identified as one farmer on a small, remote plantation called Tía Locha on the River Guasare in the state of Zulia, where he grew sixteen hectares (forty acres) of pure *criollo*. Agronomists found the Guasare cacao to be one of the purest *criollos* they had ever seen—probably an Andean strain that might have traveled north to Central America.

The scientists decided that this "old" cacao deserved to be thoroughly investigated. They collected pods at Tía Locha and brought them back to the Campo Experimental San Juan de Lagunillas, the agricultural experimental station headed by Gladys Ramos Carranza close to the Andean city of Mérida, a center of research for various crops. The Guasare cacao was planted and grown out like the *porcelana* at Chama (less than a couple of hours away), the only difference being that the climate in Mérida is semidry and the land sandy and rocky. The seedlings were unusually precocious, blossoming at two years and bearing at three—a clear advantage over slower-maturing varieties. Even more tempting for growers was the expert's estimate that at full maturity (about six years), Guasare trees planted at 3- by 3-meter intervals could potentially deliver 1,500 kilos (18,000 pounds) of cacao per hectare (2.5 acres) in a year.

LEFT: Newly planted Guasare seedlings from San Juan de Lagunillas thrive at the Finca San Joaquín in the Venezuelan plains. Rather than starting the Guasare field from scratch, agronomist Beatriz Escobar opted for the *cultivo de monte,* or the clearing of the underbrush and the planting of seedlings under the protective shade of existing tall trees. Two years later, the trees were already bearing blossoms. BELOW: Red and green Guasare pods in different stages of ripeness next to plump freshly harvested beans. At San Juan de Lagunillas, Gladys Ramos Carranza ferments the beans in small sweat boxes and dries them in the sun to make chocolate samples.

Guasare pods are imposing, some larger than thirteen inches. They exhibit the characteristic warty *cundeamor* shape with a discreet bottleneck and slightly curved tip. There are red and green Guasares. The latter range from grass green to deep olive green, turning greenish yellow when fully mature. The red type is a stunning cabernet red when immature, ripening to a burnt orange. The beans are large, plump, and pure white inside. Their quality is extraordinary. The chocolate I sampled made from well-fermented Guasare at a manufacturer's lab in 1995 was fantastic—everyone in our tasting panel found it even more flavorful and complex than the even-keeled *porcelana*.

A rain-soaked immature Guasare pod in the Venezuelan Andes

Soon growers from every cacao region of Venezuela were coming in droves to the nursery at the Mérida station, looking for Guasare pods and stock to plant as their star cacao. Interestingly, so far it seems sturdy and productive in different environments, even at the high-altitude testing area at Mérida (3,500 feet/1,066 meters). It seems to have appeared on the scene at just the right moment to attract notice from some of the world's top chocolatiers—certainly it will be showing up in premium European and U.S. chocolates.

THE NEW TASTE OF CHOCOLATE

## ANDEAN CRIOLLOS FROM MÉRIDA

In 1900, a thriving colonial plantation in Mérida state called La Molina had 740 acres (300 hectares) planted with *criollo* cacao so pure it only required twenty-four hours to be fully fermented. The plantation produced an average yield of 200 *quintales* (about 20,000 pounds) yearly. The area even had its own denomination of origin, "Cacao de Estanquez," and it was taken down to the port of Gibraltar in Sur del Lago to be shipped with *porcelana* and other *criollos* to the larger international port of Maracaibo. By the 1930s the plantation had gone over to sugarcane, and little remained of the once flourishing *criollo* trees. Only the tiered drying yards and a practical rail system to transport cacao in wagons speak of its former life. This seems to summa-

rize the commercial history of cacao throughout the Venezuelan Andes.

Today there are only isolated pockets of *criollos* of various phenotypes *(cundeamor, angoleta, porcelana)* in many Andean communities. Some of the most fascinating specimens have been found growing as ornamentals near farmhouses. Scattered *criollos* can also be found on most working plantations where *trinitarios* and the now ubiquitous *pajarito* from Colombia prevail.

Gladys Ramos Carranza has begun collecting specimens of pure Andean *criollos* and planting them in a plot at her experimental station. Shown here is a pure *criollo* hybrid with the characteristic smooth skin and the telling nipplelike tip imprint of *porcelana* and large, plump, white seeds.

## THEOBROMA PENTAGONA

The most exotic of the western Venezuelan cacaos, and the one that has caused the most head scratching by geneticists, is something that people didn't originally know was cacao at all. Decades ago, the literature used to describe it as another species, *Theobroma pentagona,* found growing wild (or semiwild) in Central America. But about ten years ago specimens growing in a semiwild state were discovered on a few scattered farms in the *criollo andino* territory of Venezuela. They are now considered to be a true cacao and have been reclassified as *Theobroma cacao* var. *pentagona.*

The pods of this odd-looking cacao have five sharply defined ridges that recall the folded angular wings of a fruit bat, and the whole pod seems to erupt with lumpy warts, as if some primeval animal was hatching within and getting ready to burst forth. This cacao has the characteristic thin skin of *criollos* and contains fifteen to twenty beans that are large and plump.

The *pentagona* story is only beginning to be written. Is it native to Venezuela? Was it brought to that country from Central America? Is it truly a wild cacao? Is it a surviving relative of some ancient *criollo,* or perhaps an ancestor that interbred with another species to produce the *criollo* race? Does it have potential as a hybridizer? These questions may not be answered any time soon. However, what the agronomists are certain of, as in the study of other important food plants like corn, is that the existence of wild or semiwild relatives opens up the past as part of the future. Somewhere within the DNA of these plants may lie clues as to their innate survival strategies in terms of pollination patterns, climatic adaptability, and resistance to natural enemies. With any crop as fragile and often besieged as *criollo* cacao, any rich source of genetic insight is a well-timed miracle.

LEFT: This red, warty *Theobroma pentagona* pod comes from an isolated tree grown as an ornamental in the home of Eulogio Contreras in the town of Hernández in Táchira state, on the Venezuelan-Colombian border. The beans of this cacao are large and plump and show a more pronounced purple hue than would be characteristic of red-skinned *porcelana.*

OPPOSITE, BOTTOM: On the religious feast of Corpus Christi, masked dancers known as Los Diablitos ("the Little Devils") parade the main road of the town of Chuao to the sound of drums. The dancers are cacao workers belonging to La Sociedad de Corpus, an all-male religious confraternity.

## CENTRAL VENEZUELAN CRIOLLOS

The strikingly beautiful river valleys of Venezuela's central coastal highlands in the state of Aragua—Choroní, Chuao, Cata, Ocumare, Cuyagua—are nestled between tall mountains that plunge abruptly into the Caribbean Sea. The names of some of the most coveted cacaos in the world still resound in these fertile oases, where relics of the

*criollo* cacao, believed to have been brought to Venezuela from Nicaragua or the Nicoya Peninsula in Costa Rica in the early colonial period, still survive. Here also live the descendants of Africans brought as slaves, most probably from Angola, to work on some of the finest plantations in the world.

During carnival and religious festivities, such as Corpus Christi and Saint John's Eve in June, the valleys explode with the sounds of Africa. For a few frantic days, the sounds of the plantation routine drawing to its second annual peak are replaced by something as old as the Venezuelan cacao trade. Religious rites, songs, and dances that once were an integral part of the life of the African slaves are reenacted in a secular context.

Recurrent outbreaks of cacao disease starting in the nineteenth century meant the introduction of sturdy *trinitarios,* which the Venezuelans called *forasteros* ("alien," "nonnative") to the confusion of modern observers who think that *forastero* refers only to Amazonian cacao. Because of more than a century of hybridization between *criollos* and *trinitarios* (followed by the ill-advised introduction of *amelonados* and other *forasteros* at a later period), the percentage of pure *criollos* found in these valleys fluctuates widely. Venezuelan scientists classify these extant *criollos* as "modern criollos" *(criollos actuales)* to set them apart from the "old *criollos"* such as *porcelana* and Guasare, native to Venezuela.

## Choroní

A century ago, Choroní meant cacao. Today the name conjures up vacation time and scantily clad German and Canadian tourists getting to know the locals "intimately." This once-thriving cacao region has

succumbed to its own tropical charms. Small hostels and hotels have sprung everywhere, and carnival time attracts throngs of beer-drinking revelers who clog the narrow mountain road and fill the streets near the port.

Close to the coast, the mountains are dry, covered with mixed cactus growth. But seen from above, a broad meandering green snake seems to cut its way toward the sea. This is the Choroní River, which runs through a narrow valley lush with cacao and its motherly shade trees.

The dignified old town, Santa Clara de Choroní, with its white houses trimmed in colonial blue and its ancient wooden doors, is a striking contrast to the garish tourist town that has sprung up near the port. Only a few cacao plantations remain—the loveliest of all, La Sabaneta. This restored colonial beauty has hundreds of acres planted with cacao. Walking through its many sectors is like getting lost in a genetic maze where you occasionally find your bearings by spotting an old *criollo* tree with red, warty, deeply furrowed red pods sporting a curved pointy tip. This is the heart of old Choroní. The pulp is good to eat and the pods have a high percentage of plump white beans, betraying their strong *criollo* germplasm.

Two factors have contributed to the demise of this wonderful *criollo:* tourism, which draws workers to the hotel industry and away from the cacao tree, and disease, which has been a constant threat since at least the nineteenth century. Many pods look healthy, but when you cut them open, you find the seeds ravaged by disease. The scourge of Choroní is the deadly *Ceratocystis fimbriata,* a fungal disease known as *mal de Choroní* (Choroní disease or cocoa wilt), which can kill cacao overnight.

TOP, CENTER: A cacao worker examines a Choroní pod. RIGHT: Ancient shade trees loom like a mantle over the thick cacao groves of the eighteenth-century Hacienda La Sabaneta. Kai Rosenberg, the owner of this colonial beauty, is intent on revitalizing *criollo* cacao in Choroní. Together with four other local growers, Rosenberg is collaborating with scientists from FONAIAP (Fondo Nacional de Investigaciones Agropecuarias) to combat cacao diseases and improve productivity.

## Chuao

Merchants in France and Spain always spoke of Chuao cacao as one of the finest that could be had for the money, and they paid high premiums for the prestigious beans. Even today European manufacturers jockey to corner the whole production of the area's only farm, meager though it has become in the last decades (ranging from eight or nine metric tons a year to an alleged fourteen metric tons in 1999).

Chuao was always one of the most isolated Venezuelan cacao estates, reachable only by boat from the nearby coastal valley of Choroní. Naturally it has resisted most kinds of visible change. The faces of the people reflect those of residents in the seventeenth century, and the same few surnames (Liendo, Bolívar) testify to the early history of the hacienda.

What has changed is the quality of the cacao. At the beginning of the nineteenth century, Chuao cacao was a pure and most delicate *criollo.* But the diseases that attacked *criollo* cacao elsewhere caught up with even remote Chuao. The threatened groves were replanted first with *trinitario* strains that were less vulnerable but had good flavor. Through the years, however, inferior *forasteros* were used to replace older or diseased *criollo* and *trinitario* trees. Just walking through some sectors of the plantation, you see typical long, warty *criollo* pods with the characteristic hooked tip of the *cundeamor* type alternating with round, shiny specimens that anyone familiar with cacao would recognize at once as *amelonado,* one of the most common *forasteros.* A batch of freshly harvested beans appears large and promising at first glance, but on cutting them open you find that they exhibit every color between pure white and deep purple. This means that the farmers are working with such a mixture of cacaos that one fermentation approach can't do justice to any of them, much less all of them. Still, bring a bunch of dried Chuao beans close to your nose. In this now-natural blend of varying quality cacaos, the perfume of *criollo* still flutters like a brightly colored banner.

ABOVE, RIGHT: A ripe pod displays the characteristic warty *cundeamor* shape, pronounced bottleneck, and slightly curved tip. It contains plump beans with pure white and light pink cotyledons of a true Chuao *criollo.* LEFT: Boats ferry passengers along the rugged coast of the state of Aragua to inaccessible towns such as Chuao.

## LONG LIVE THE CACAO OF CHUAO!

The famous Venezuelan plantation of Chuao on the central Caribbean coast was originally a royal *encomienda* (land grant) given to an aristocratic Spanish family in 1592, and worked by Africans brought as slaves. When the surviving heir, Doña Catalina Mexía de Liendo, died in 1669, she donated the plantation to the Franciscan friars as a charitable gift and stipulated that "my slaves" should go along with the property, enabling them to remain together and to continue forging a bond with the land.

The Franciscans owned Chuao until 1827, by which time Venezuela had won independence from Spain. Simón Bolívar, the "Liberator," donated the hacienda to the University of Caracas, which retained ownership for several generations, eventually handing over the plantation to the Venezuelan government in 1883. First it was sold to the dictator Antonio Guzmán Blanco, then it was shunted from one political racketeer to another for about eighty years. Finally it came under the aegis of the state and the control of the ill-fated Fondo Nacional del Cacao, organized in the 1960s as a government monopoly of all Venezuelan cacao. The Fondo Nacional turned over the management of the farm to the workers, and Chuao became a cooperative of about 740 acres (300 hectares). And so in a rare instance of historical justice, it has come to be governed by the descendants of the same slaves who had been "given" to the Franciscan order by Doña Catalina three centuries before. The women still sing to Catalina while they dry the beans in the courtyard of the church: *El cacao de Chuao, ¡que viva que viva! Que Catalina lo fundó, lo fundó* (Long live the cacao of Chuao that Catalina founded!).

OPPOSITE, INSET: A sample of beans from Chuao's only fermentation facility shows a rainbow of cotyledon colors—from ivory white (after oxidation) to light pink to deep purple—a sign of the genetic diversity of the contemporary cacao plantation.

ABOVE: Oliver Bolívar (left, front) and friends
LEFT: Pancho Bolívar returns from the fields on the cooperative's tractor.

## Ocumare

The inaccessible Ocumare de la Costa is another lovely valley on the central coast of Venezuela. There *criollo* cacao has undergone a severe process of hybridization, but cacao still remains viable as a commercial crop. Though yields are very low, cacao from Ocumare and the equally remote neighboring valley Cuyagua (which has similar cacao) often reaches the world market as a single-origin specialty cacao and is sold for a hefty premium.

In the 1940s, a group of Venezuelan scientists made a selection of healthy and productive *criollo* trees in Ocumare and numbered them for reference. The marvelous cacao shown here, with classic *cundeamor* shape and lovely hues of pink, is the selection Ocumare 61. Select clones such as this have been planted all over Venezuela, because they have proven to be vigorous and flavorful. When you cut open a pod, you find very large and plump beans with cotyledons that range from pure white to light pink to light purple.

Ocumare 61 is the predominant cacao in the new San Joaquín Estate chocolate made by El Rey. San Joaquín is a gutsy, earthy chocolate with peachy fruitiness and a floral bouquet. Most of these flavor notes plus a very subtle dairy note can be attributed to Ocumare 61.

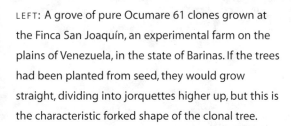

LEFT: A grove of pure Ocumare 61 clones grown at the Finca San Joaquín, an experimental farm on the plains of Venezuela, in the state of Barinas. If the trees had been planted from seed, they would grow straight, dividing into jorquettes higher up, but this is the characteristic forked shape of the clonal tree.

OPPOSITE: A prime specimen of Ocumare 61 at the Finca San Joaquín

## Forasteros

Geneticists have found various wrinkles and puzzles within the *forastero* tribe. But to simplify greatly, they now identify two main groups of *forastero:* Upper Amazon and Lower Amazon, named for their areas of origin in the river basin. These sturdy *forasteros* are the workhorses and warriors of the cacao tribe, called on to increase a farm's overall productivity while making it less vulnerable to the diseases that attack other cacaos. They provide manufacturers with the most inexpensive, general common-denominator beans and bulk beans that deliver clean chocolate flavor.

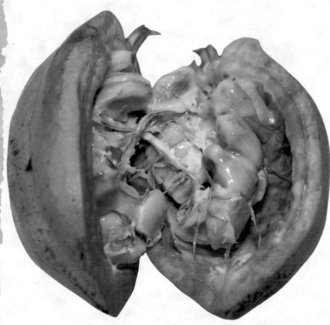

A *forastero* pod collected at La Pagerie, a former sugar estate, on the Caribbean island of Martinique

## LOWER AMAZON FORASTEROS

One cacao type stands as the emblem of the international cacao boom at the beginning of the twentieth century: *amelonado,* a *forastero* whose handsome, often smooth-skinned fruits have a typical melonlike shape. *Amelonado* is the archetypal Lower Amazon *forastero* cacao, probably native to the area of eastern Brazil that is now the state of Pará. While genetically distinct from its relatives in the Upper Amazon, it shares with them the same feisty vigor and the characteristic flat seeds with deep purple cotyledons.

*Amelonado* seems to be the uninvited guest at every party, popping up next to pure *criollos* and showing up—most likely as a workhorse—in many large commercial plantations. It is the cacao Tabasco farmers carry to church, hanging from poles, to be blessed on the feast day of San Isidro. It is also the source of the unfermented flat, tan Tabasco beans that Mexican buyers often prefer to darker fermented beans from Chiapas. You can walk through plantations from the Dominican Republic to Martinique, from Bahia to Nigeria, and recognize the characteristic shape of this Amazonian native. Though most *amelonado* pods are green ripening to yellow, there are also red *amelonados.*

*Amelonado* is capable of great finesse when it is properly cared for and fermented for the right number of days. Sun-drying on mats, as is done in West Africa, seems to be a factor in helping to mellow this cacao, which often misbehaves and tastes acrid and acid in its native Amazonian habitat.

ABOVE, LEFT: A Honduran woman of Mayan ancestry holds an *amelonado* pod, grown in a small farm in the Aldea Toyo not far from San Pedro Sula. The pulp of this cacao is vinegary and the beans small, flat, and deep purple.

ABOVE, RIGHT: Unfermented beans drying in the sun on the highway between San Pedro Sula and Tela. Though their external color is light terra-cotta, the cotyledons within remain a deep purple after drying.

In this picture taken at Ghana's Cocoa Research Institute, *amelonado* (left) is seen with other types of cacao grown at the institute.

## UPPER AMAZON FORASTEROS

*In order to get a proper perspective on Amazon valley cacao, it must be realized that the trees are not shaded in the way Trinidad and Colombian cacao is. Large areas up to several acres may occur without a single shade tree but generally mixed with the cacao there do occur an occasional breadfruit (Artocarpus incisa), Brazil nut (Berthowetia excelsa), cedar (Cedrela mexicana), or mango tree all of which provide some shade. Another feature about this cacao is that as in Ecuador it rarely extends far from the river bank. Usually it is limited to about 2–3 hundred yards back from the river and for this reason the cacao grown is probably not indigenous to the site where it occurs. The trees are often large and multiple trunked due to the profusion of basal chupons which are never cut away. The canopy is always dense because no pruning is done and where trees occur in groups the canopy forms such an interlaced tangle that few weeds grow in the soil beneath.*

F. J. POUND (1938)

Every food plant has its Indiana Jones, and for Upper Amazon *forasteros,* the hero was F. J. Pound, a brilliant geneticist working at the Imperial College of Tropical Agriculture in Trinidad. Between 1937 and 1938, Pound traveled to Ecuador and through the Amazon River basin to collect pods and budwood of wild cacao showing resistance to witches' broom disease.

Pound paints a dismal picture in the report of his 1938 expedition. He found the disease well established everywhere, from the ornamental cacao growing right next to infected *cupuaçu* trees at the zoological garden of Belém to the wild or semiwild cacao of the headwaters of the Amazon River. In the end, however, Pound found what he was looking for: pockets of healthy *forastero* trees showing vigorous growth amid diseased trees.

From the headwaters of the Amazon to Ecuador and then Colombia, Pound collected important resistant specimens that he sent to Trinidad's quarantine station in Barbados, where more than one thousand rootstocks had

In appearance most Upper Amazon cacaos are unprepossessing. IMC (Iquitos Mixed Calabacillo) pods from the Peruvian Amazon are smallish and nearly monochromatic, a dull green that becomes orange-yellow as it matures.

THE NEW TASTE OF CHOCOLATE

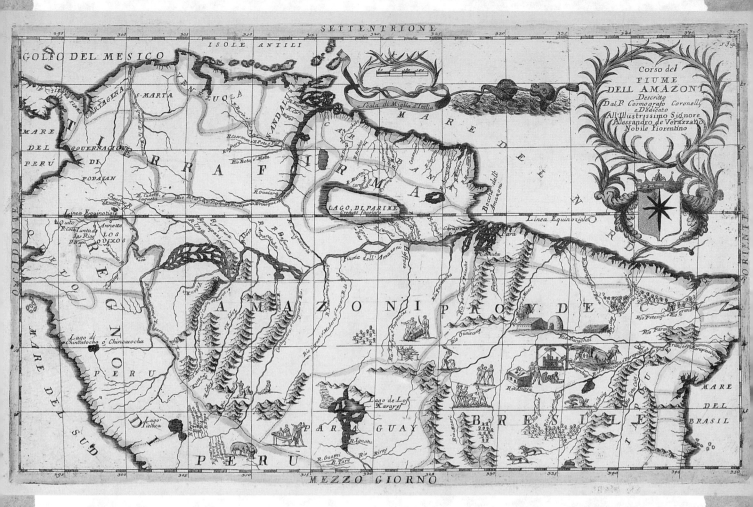

ABOVE: *Corso del Fiume dell Amazoni* by Vincenzo Coronelli, 1691/1695. This Amazon basin map extends from Panama to Brazil and includes the mythical Lake Parime, the site of El Dorado, between the Guiana coast and the Amazon. Shown in the interior are many curious scenes of Indian life, including a village and farm field, Indians harvesting sugar cane and operating a mill, an Indian battle, and scenes of cannibalism.

The junction of the Rio Negro and the Amazon River

IDENTIFYING CACAO

been prepared. The collected specimens were planted at Marper Farm, the Manhattan Project of cacao research, where the stock was exposed to witches' broom to test its resistance. The most resilient trees were then crossed with each other or with some chosen Imperial College Selection trees. The stars of the Marper experiment were several lines of IMCs (Iquitos Mixed Calabacillo) from the Iquitos Marañon River area, and the Peruvian Scavina, Nanay, and Parinari selections—all named after particular areas or rivers.

In later years, new genetic materials from the Peruvian and Ecuadorian Amazon as well as Colombia were obtained by expeditions sponsored by the Imperial College of Tropical Agriculture. These enriched the collection of the Imperial College (later called the University of the West Indies in St. Augustine) in Trinidad, culminating in the creation of the world's largest germplasm bank (ICG, T) with close to three thousand accessions. DNA analysis reveals that Upper Amazon cacaos show more genetic variability than Lower Amazon *forasteros*.

Three Upper Amazon selections from the International Cocoa Genebank, Trinidad (ICG, T)

London Cacao Trade/Estación Experimental Napo (LCT/EEN), an Ecuadorian *forastero* collected by the London Cacao Trade Amazonian expedition

Pound 78, a Peruvian *forastero* collected by Pound in 1943

Nanay 399 (name carved by scientist on husk), one of fourteen disease-resistant cacaos collected by Pound in the Peruvian Amazon

THE NEW TASTE OF CHOCOLATE

LEFT: Darin Sukha, a researcher at the Cocoa Research Unit in Trinidad, cuts a Nanay 406 pod from the International Cocoa Genebank of Trinidad to study back at CRU. RIGHT: A hand-pollinated cacao flower protected by a net. The flowers of *criollo* cacao are capable of self-pollination. But Upper Amazon *forasteros* and some *trinitarios* have a condition called self-incompatibility, which can prevent the flowers from being fertilized by their own pollen. In any case, the fruit is more viable when pollinated by another plant. Certain midges are better able than other insects to crawl into the flowers and bring the pollen to the ovary. On some plantations and research institutes, pollination is carried out by hand to ensure that particular crosses between select stock are not ruined by cacao's inherent promiscuity.

## THE SCIENCE OF CACAO

Agronomist Julie Reneau, a researcher for Nestlé, prepares leaf samples. Leaf tissue cut from a wide variety of cacao trees at the International Cocoa Genebank of Trinidad will be inoculated with the fungus that causes black pod rot. In two or three days, signs of infection begin to appear on the leaf issue as dark spots. Unblemished samples reveal resistance to disease. After further testing, these cacaos, mostly Upper Amazon *forasteros* and select hybrids, will eventually be used for grafting and sent to breeding programs abroad.

### IMC 67

You'll find this sturdy cacao in many breeding programs where cacao is grown with little shade and where witches' broom or *Ceratocystis fimbriata* (cocoa wilt) are endemic. When crossed with *criollos,* IMC 67 lends vigor as well as fruitiness. This Peruvian *forastero* is a good producer (about forty-five flat, dark purple beans per pod) and is often found as a cultivar in commercial plantations across the world from Grenada to Kona Estate in Hawaii.

### Scavina 6

If I were to choose only one type of cacao for eating as a fruit, it would be the Scavina, an Ecuadorian *forastero.* (The squirrels of Trinidad also prefer it to any other cacao.) The pulp of the Scavina 6 is sweet, fruity, complex, and floral—as perfumed as passion fruit juice. With its known resistance to witches' broom, Scavina 6 adds a floral quality and pleasant fruitiness to chocolate. Its robust purple beans also contribute a note of bitterness. Of all Upper Amazon *forasteros,* this is the closest in aroma to the coveted Ecuadorian Arriba.

Scavina can be found all over the world as parent stock in several hybrids or as a cultivar in its own right. In Bahia, Scavina 6 was crossed with the *trinitario* selection ICS 1 from Trinidad to form a cacao known in the trade as Theobahia, which has proven resistant to disease.

### Scavina 12

A rougher, more pronounced, ridged husk distinguishes this variety from its close relative Scavina 6. The beans are characteristically flat with deep purple cotyledons. The pulp is not as fruity or perfumed as that of Scavina 6.

## A SPECIAL CACAO: ARRIBA

Arriba is one of the more coveted *forastero* cacaos. To reach their potential, the beans need an unusually short fermentation. This makes them unsuitable to throw in as part of a mixed *forastero* batch. Despite fervent efforts by growers, none of Arriba's unique floral fragrance ever develops when it is planted anywhere outside its ecological niche in Ecuador.

Arriba trees are very tall and large, though they are less productive than *trinitarios* and *forasteros*. The thick-husked pods exhibit features of both *amelonado* and *cundeamor* cacao, with a suggestion of a bottleneck and a furrowed, often warty surface. The beans range in color from pale to deep purple. Arriba beans are fermented briefly, sometimes less than twenty-four hours, for the optimum development of their characteristic floral perfume.

### MYSTERIOUS LINEAGE

An aura of mystery surrounds the Scavina, which is often listed as either a Peruvian or Ecuadorian *forastero*. Antonio Figuera, a Brazilian scientist, believes it was collected by Pound at the Fundo Monte Blanco, a farm on the left margin of the Ucayali River in Peru that was owned by an Eduardo Scavino. Analysis by the so-called RAPD (randomly amplified polymorphic DNA) technique for detecting genetic "fingerprints" reveals that Scavina is indeed genetically related to other cacaos from this region.

This Arriba specimen was collected by cacao expert Silvio Crespo decades ago from an old tree in Pueblo Viejo, Ecuador.

Pueblo Viejo, Ecuador, from *South America, Sheet 1: Ecuador, Granada, Venezuela* by Humboldt and Codazzi, 1846

## Trinitarios

Trinidad is the Noah's ark of cacao—a vessel holding the most complete genetic reservoir of the hybrid cacao we know today as *trinitario*. Cacao conservation in Trinidad began in the 1920s under the auspices of the Imperial College of Tropical Agriculture. Memories of the genetic catastrophe suffered by the island in the eighteenth century together with the ever-present threat of diseases such as black pod rot and witches' broom prompted geneticists and botanists to begin a systematic classification and selection of the best genetic material available on the island.

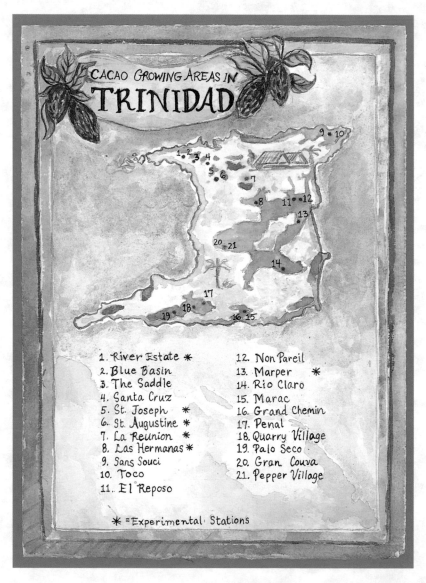

A map of Trinidad's cacao growing regions and experimental cacao fields (after a map by Frances Bekele of Trinidad's Cocoa Research Unit)

THE NEW TASTE OF CHOCOLATE

## IMPERIAL COLLEGE SELECTIONS 1 TO 100

In 1933, the geneticist F. J. Pound under the supervision of the botanist E. E. Cheesman selected one thousand trees from farms all over the island. The criteria for selection were high productivity and resistance to disease. Further testing narrowed the selection to one hundred clones, which formed the core of the so-called ICS (Imperial College Selections) 1 to 100. The collection and systematic study of these heirloom trees has proven invaluable for cacao researchers all over the world.

I first encountered ICS trees at the International Cacao Genebank in Trinidad. The trees have been planted over a large area, and I had to walk over rugged terrain, jumping up and down and crossing irrigation ditches to take a closer look at the few trees that were bearing ripe pods that time of the year. After walking though several lots of Upper Amazon *forasteros,* with their unimpressive smallish yellow pods, ICS 1 came as a refreshing sight. The tree had pods in all stages of growth. The pods, which varied in color from deep crimson to burnt orange, sprang from trunks and branches that sported small tags, pieces of colorful plastic twine, and notes pinned on by the scientists who have done experiments with this accession.

With an estimated production of 106 medium-sized pods a year, enclosing an average of forty-two plump, light-cotyledon beans, ICS 1 is an attractive cultivar. In sensory evaluation tests, ICS 1 liquor is described as having a mild chocolate flavor (in comparison to the West African standard) and a pronounced fruitiness. The cross of ICS 1 with

The unripe pod of ICS 1 ( ABOVE ) shows red ridges and green furrows that will later change to the uniform orange of the mature specimen ( BELOW ).

Scavina 6 is found to be highly productive and resistant to witches' broom.

Clones of the Imperial College Selection were planted in several plantations throughout the island of Trinidad. I first saw the whole collection at San Juan Estate, Philippe Agostini's lovely cacao farm near Gran Couva. The field is located uphill in a rugged section of this old farm. It is really marvelous to see all these heirloom trees together in a single field, many with the original metal identification tags still attached. It is a living document of the enormous range of pod sizes, shapes, and colors possessed by the first *trinitario* population of the island. All shades from green to yellow to purple are represented, but the predominant hue is cabernet red ripening to brilliant orange. When cut open, the beans show the full range of possible *trinitario* coloring from light pink to dark purple. Some of the pods are long and warty. Others like ICS 82 are huge, round, and smooth-skinned with large, lozenge-shaped purple beans.

ICS 82 (San Juan Estate, Trinidad)

ICS 84, a *criollo* hybrid at the International Cocoa Genebank, Trinidad

ICS 95 (unripe)

ICS 95

ICS (Imperial College Selection) clones from Trinidad have been planted on cacao farms all over the world. These large pods are specimens of ICS 95, a *trinitario* with a strong *criollo* germplasm, from Hacienda La Concepción in Barlovento, Venezuela. It has been used there in crossings with the farm's old *criollo* selections to produce more flavorful cultivars with plump seeds and thin shells that are also resistant to black pod disease.

## OCUMARE × IMC 67

The hybrids of several *criollo* selections from Ocumare de la Costa and Upper Amazon cacaos created by Dr. Lilian Reyes grow on many progressive farms throughout Venezuela, from Barinas to the Paria Peninsula. Technically they are *trinitarios* that have proven resistant to several diseases and are tolerant of poor shade. The cross between Ocumare 61 and IMC 67 (Iquitos Mixed Calabacillo) yields a full-bodied *trinitario* cacao with lots of the fruity qualities of its sturdy Upper Amazon parent and the elegant dairy notes of its *criollo* mother. This cacao forms the core of the Río Caribe cacao, the commercial name for the former Carúpano cacao. It is also the most important hybrid in San Joaquin, a progressive plantation in Barinas, in the sun-scorched plains of Venezuela.

Ocumare 61 x IMC 67 (Finca San Joaquín, Barinas State)

## TSH
## (TRINIDAD SELECT HYBRIDS)

Select ICS clones have been further hybridized with the most vigorous and disease-resistant Upper Amazon cacaos collected in Ecuador and Peru by Pound, to produce the so-called Trinidad Select Hybrids, which have been propagated all over the world.

TSH (La Reunión, Trinidad)

THE NEW TASTE OF CHOCOLATE

## VENEZUELA: HERITAGE AND FUTURE

Venezuela is a land that has always offered rare opportunities for cacao growers—but at the price of risky cash investments, struggles with nature, and tensions between the private and public sectors. The first cacao rush, which began in the seventeenth century, created a class of Creole plantation owners so lordly that they were called the *grandes cacaos* (the big cacaos). But even when strains of fine *criollo* cacao were winning Venezuela international fame, the Spanish crown and the local entrepreneurs were usually at loggerheads. The *grandes cacaos* did not take kindly to Madrid's efforts to establish a Spanish monopoly on the cacao trade. Much cacao and money surreptitiously found its way between Venezuela, the Dutch and English colonies of the Caribbean, and "New Spain" (Mexico).

Over the years, Venezuela continued to produce more *criollo* cacao than any other nation. In the early nineteenth century, outbreaks of disease prompted the introduction of sturdier *trinitarios*. This was followed by much natural hybridization, especially in the forested coastal valleys and the Barlovento area east of Caracas. Today you can still taste a marked distinction between regional cacaos from these places—which are just acid enough to develop a characteristic fruitiness—and the very low-acid, nutty-flavored *porcelana* cacao of western Venezuela. But both the *criollos* and the *trinitarios* of the country remained standards of excellence of their kind for an impressively long time.

Then came the Venezuelan oil boom of the 1920s, which sent cacao cultivation into a decline. There seemed to be faster ways of making a living, or a fortune. Somehow the local cacaos avoided the extreme genetic degradation that took place in parts of Central America, but a lot of criollo trees were cut down and replaced with very poor *forasteros*. Slovenly post-harvest treatment practices crept in. The Venezuelan government did not help matters by emulating colonial Spain and taking over the buying and selling of cacao in 1975. The state monopoly, the Fondo Nacional del Cacao, went far toward running the industry into the ground by obliterating any distinctions of quality and buying the best-treated beans at the same price as moldy or unfermented ones.

However, the government monopoly was abolished in 1991, and a handful of growers saw an opportunity to upgrade their operation and sell better cacao at better prices—especially to the up-and-coming Venezuelan chocolate industry and foreign manufacturers of fine couvertures.

These progressive growers have drawn up an agenda called "Plan Cacao," which if implemented will allocate both private and state funds for technical aid to existing cacao farms and establish guidelines for certifying quality and origin. Their boldest initiative is the proposed development of an entirely new cacao region, the vast *llanos,* or plains, of Venezuela stretching from the Andes to the Orinoco. This is not only virgin territory for cacao—the *llanos* have historically been home-on-the-range cattle country—but also totally unlike the ecosystem in which cacao has always been raised. The *llanos* are open, shadeless ground that fluctuates between seasons of rain and drought. Farming cacao here means sinking a lot of money into irrigation systems. If the venture succeeds, the reward will be an enormous expanse of newly available land, free of the usual forest-bred cacao disease, and a potential source of prosperity for the *llaneros* (plainsmen), who have fallen on hard times.

# Tasting Chocolate

People often ask me to tell them what they should look for when tasting chocolate. I can only tell them what I look for. The appreciation of chocolate is always going to be a subjective experience, to which everyone brings a smidgen (or a ton) of personal baggage and cultural or national prejudice. But we can learn to set aside our built-in biases enough to identify important elements with some objectivity.

## Chocolate Preferences

Americans in blind tastings instinctively go for blends with especially high West African cacao content. This happens to be a dominant cacao in some of the mass-produced brands most Americans have eaten since childhood. Naturally it is identified with full chocolate flavor (perhaps also because it has an echo of the *robusta*-type coffees that show up on most of our breakfast tables). On the other hand, Germans tend to hate the intense extra bitter chocolate adored in France. Americans gravitate to very light and French people to very dark milk chocolate. The Swiss and the Japanese go hand in hand in their love for buttery, high-fat, slick, and satiny chocolate.

There are no rights or wrongs with such penchants. We can't necessarily erase the parts of our sensory memory, but to some extent we can separate what we really taste from what we want to taste or imagine we are tasting. Without turning the act of enjoying chocolate into a pretentious ritual, we can sharpen our perceptions enough to take them seriously and to form real judgments. Not all chocolates are born equal, and not all cacaos deserve to be processed into chocolate. Cacao is a noble plant, but some strains are better off back in the jungle or in a germplasm bank helping to preserve the biodiversity of cacao.

119

## How to Test Taste

When I taste chocolate for professional purposes, I like to do it as a comparative process with no more than half a dozen chocolates of similar cacao content from several manufacturers. I don't like mixing chocolates with varying degrees of sweetness or milk and dark chocolates in the same sensory evaluation test. The goal is to concentrate on chocolate's intrinsic qualities without being distracted by differing sugar contents or dairy components that mask some flavors and enhance others. In tasting chocolate for your own enjoyment or education (or both), try to focus on things legitimately connected with taste.

Some companies have developed their own particular language, which they teach their customers, to talk about the flavor and aroma of a chocolate. For the most part, the standard language of chocolate tasting is very much like the language used in wine tasting. I think you will get more from trying to express your sensations in your own words. There is no need to be baroque when describing chocolate flavors. Draw from your experiences. Think of broad categories of flavor: acid, bitter, astringent, sweet. Make connections with everyday flavors: the fruitiness of raisins or prunes, the nutty and buttery flavor of macadamia nuts or the sweeter but more interesting taste of cashews, the tang of cooked cherries, the musky taste of bitter almond in marzipan, the mild astringency of a green fruit or a banana peel. Try to recall the smell of the foods you like (such as freshly baked bread or pungent cheeses) or the aroma of nature itself: flowery, herbal, spicy. Remember the smell of a gush of rain on hot street pavement, the tempting scent of ripening fruit, or the disturbing pungency of slightly rotten fruit.

Look for what appeals to you in the chocolates you taste, but also take notes on those elements of flavor and taste that offend you. Here is the way I approach every single chocolate I taste.

### COLOR

I first examine the chocolates visually for color cues that might help me identify the provenance of the beans. But here you need to dismiss the commonly held notion that dark chocolates are best. Some *trinitarios* and *criollos,* particularly those from the Indian Ocean, have light brown cotyledons that result in light reddish brown chocolate. Thus some chocolates, such as Valrhona's Manjari, melt with the rich color of copper. Many *forasteros* are very dark, but others are a pleasant medium-rich brown. Excellent-quality *trinitarios* might range from light brown to dark brown, and some *trinitarios* grown in Malaysia are darker in color than West African *amelonados,* which are preferred for milk chocolates.

I also look for other external cues such as a "bloom," which is an ashy coating on the surface of the bar. Chocolate bloom is often a sign of poor storage, not poor quality. When cacao is subject to drastic changes of temperature, it loses its "temper," which means that some of the cacao butter crystals have fallen out of alignment and risen to the surface of the bar, forming a bloom.

## AROMAS

I start tasting by breaking off a small piece of chocolate. To sample the chocolate, I first rub it between my thumb and my index finger to warm it up and help release volatile aromatic components. With one hand, I take the chocolate to my nose and sniff it, while cupping the other hand over it. This is your first chance to separate out the different aspects of a complex sensation. Do not underestimate the sense of smell. It is intimately connected with the way we perceive flavors. To prove this point, place a piece of chocolate in your mouth and pinch your nose. You might identify bitter, sweet, salty, or sour sensations, and even get to enjoy the cooling touch of chocolate on your tongue, but you will not be able to explore the manifold nuances of flavor, because you can't smell them.

## Undesirable Smells

What does the chocolate smell like? I first look for undesirable odors. These are mostly the result of poor post-harvest treatment of the cacao bean or the inherent aroma of certain poor-quality beans. Some unfermented or artificially dried *forasteros* smell like burnt rubber or plastic. Cacao has a knack for absorbing odors. When cacao is stored in humid conditions, it can absorb the grassy odor of the burlap bag. Cacao beans dried over wood fires have a smoky scent that the trade characterizes as "hammy." I like to use such beans in cooking and in cacao and spice blends, but when turned into chocolate, they overwhelm other desirable aromas. While overfermented beans give chocolate the smell of rotting fruit, moldy beans impart a disagreeable stale odor.

## Desirable Aromas

Next, I fully concentrate on desirable aromas. Your first impression might be just "chocolatey." Keep concentrating and see what other characteristics emerge. Perhaps the basic chocolate aroma is rather dim or very intense. Perhaps it hits you all at once or seems to build. It may be accompanied by a floral sensation, a hint of ripe fruit, a slight suggestion of caramel. Some chocolates smell like freshly baked apple pie, others like luscious caramel toffee.

## TASTE

Now I taste the chocolate. The natural temptation to judge by texture and mouth feel is not the same as analyzing flavors, so try to focus on flavor.

## Chocolate Flavor

When I first bite into the chocolate, I let a little fragment rest and dissolve on my tongue for about twenty seconds. My initial intent is to measure the length of the chocolate experience. Where does the chocolate bang begin—at the beginning, the middle, or the end? Some brands have a slow start, but the flavor of chocolate blooms and mounts in a crescendo, and then lingers in your mouth. The trade describes this desirable sensation as a long finish. Some chocolates have an overpowering roast coffee flavor, which might be an indication that they have been made with unfermented beans and have been overroasted to compensate for their lack of chocolate flavor. In others, the chocolate flavor is short-lived. It might come in with a roar, but it disappears quickly.

It could be safely generalized that fine "flavor beans" have a long finish. West African cacao is known for an even, monochromatic chocolate flavor experience with a short finish and no highs or lows.

## Flavor Characterization

In tasting, we experience natural flavors and manmade flavors at once in no fixed order. In something as complex as chocolate, those flavors are bound to merge into each other. I look first for added ingredients: vanilla, salt, malt, cocoa powder, the dairy product in the milk chocolate.

Real vanilla is never overpowering. What vanilla does is both intensify and tame all other flavors, coaxing them to behave in harmony. Vanillin, which tends to be overused in some blends, is too assertive and cloyingly sweet. It always tastes artificial and leaves a bitter aftertaste. It masks other flavors, perhaps undesirable ones—which explains its indiscriminate use by some chocolate makers.

Many manufacturers use a pinch of salt to round off the flavor of milk chocolate. Powdered malt cereal is often added to milk chocolates to give a mellower caramel undertone to the blend. The Japanese prefer their milk chocolate with malt. To me, a successful milk chocolate is one in which the milk blends in seamlessly with the chocolate to create one whole integrated flavor. Many manufacturers believe that an even cacao with low acidity is best for a milk chocolate, and therefore they use West African cacao. But I think a fruity cacao with floral notes offers a counterpoint to the inherent sweetness of milk and creates a more exciting contrast. Cocoa powder is sometimes added to a particular blend to add strength to the chocolate and to boost up the cacao content, but it often leaves behind a metallic aftertaste.

## Natural Flavors

Then I try to get down to the innate qualities of the beans. Again, there may be a more slowly developed general flavor impact. The chocolate flavor of well-handled West African beans is plain and direct, and actually has become the standard against which other singular cacaos are compared. As you taste, try to focus on the natural chocolate flavors: nuttiness, acidity, fruitiness, bitterness, astringency.

Nuttiness is typical of chocolates made with pure Venezuelan *criollos* like *porcelana* and, to a certain extent, Andean *criollos.* An especially crucial variable is acidity. Too much makes a chocolate sour, but without acidity, a chocolate can be monotonous. The right level of acidity enlivens chocolate with a suggestion of fruit or wine, something associated with the best *trinitario* varieties and some Upper Amazon cacaos. Of all Venezuelan cacaos, the Carenero from Barlovento is the fruitiest. "Fruity" is one of the adjectives that first comes to mind when tasting exclusive-derivation chocolates made with Carenero beans like El Rey's Carenero Superior premium couvertures and Chocovic's Ocumare. In blends with high percentages like in Scharffen Berger chocolate, we detect a pronounced fruitiness that is reinforced by other equally fruity beans, such as Papua New Guinea or Madagascar beans. The latter have been described as having a fresh citrus flavor as opposed to the more complex flavor of "brown fruit," a trade term for effects reminiscent of raisins, prunes, or dried cherries.

In some chocolates made with a blend of fine flavor beans, we might detect floral notes of jasmine and roses. Any chocolate made with a small percentage of Arriba will have a floral component. Dairy flavor can be detected in dark chocolates made with beans from some coastal plantations of Venezuela close to Puerto Cabello. In some blends, we can identify a subtle but lingering bitter almond undertaste that I find very appealing. This is a flavor developed during fermentation.

A chocolate can also be described as winy. When you taste some fermented *trinitario* beans from Venezuela, the initial sensation is that of having tasted a still tannic cabernet with great promise. Some Venezuelan *criollos,* on the other hand, are so low in tannins or astringency that they taste like a hazelnut or macadamia nut.

When I taste chocolate I let my senses guide me, but I also look for memory cues and try to measure the chocolate against the West African standard of flavor. What are the predominant beans in this blend? *Forasteros* from West Africa, Asia, or Latin America? *Criollos* or *trinitarios,* or a blend of all these beans? I expect that chocolate tasting will become a more holistic experience when cacao beans and nibs that have been identified by origin reach the U.S. retail markets (as has happened with coffee beans). This will enable more people to use the origin as a point of reference in learning to discriminate among the many complex flavors in chocolate.

## PHILIPPE CONTICINI'S FLAVOR EXPERIMENT

Putting together a tasting of many different chocolates is one way to begin schooling yourself in the flavor complexities of chocolate. But what of learning to register interactions between chocolate and other flavors? The Parisian pastry chef Philippe Conticini has devised a brilliant lesson planned around a chocolate mousse and some neutral-tasting prop to put it on, for example bite-sized squares of angel food cake or brioche. These are served with about a dozen small bowls of sweet or savory flavorings to be sprinkled on the mousse, from sea salt to nutmeg. Everyone puts a dollop of the mousse on a piece of cake or brioche and adds a pinch of any preferred "condiment."

Conticini conducts this clever exercise a bit like a "reading," diagnosing some facet of your personality from your choice, perhaps choosing for you depending on the sense he gets of the real you. He uses a mousse made with Valrhona's Manjari chocolate, his favorite. The fruitiness of Manjari does work beautifully, but you may prefer chocolate with some other distinctive quality, or perhaps one with a plainer basic chocolate flavor (from West African or Dominican Republic cacao). The important thing is a mousse with a premium dark bittersweet chocolate.

Round up a collection of interesting little dishes for the "condiments" and use any eight to a dozen that you prefer from the following list of suggestions. It not only makes wonderful party entertainment but provides dazzling insight into the challenge of chocolate to the palate, its capacity to be many things to many people. I suggest using about 1 ounce each of the dried spices, 2 or more ounces of the sugar and coconut.

Cracked black peppercorns (preferably from Sumatra)

Cracked green peppercorns

Cracked pink peppercorns

Ground true Ceylon cinnamon  (see page 154)

Ground cassia (sold as "cinnamon" in this country)

Freshly grated nutmeg

Ground allspice

Aniseeds

Cumin seeds

Ground cardamom

Ground ginger

Dried lavender blossoms

Grated Indonesian or Indian palm sugar

Grated Latin American brown loaf sugar (called piloncillo, panela, papelón)

Coarse sea salt

Ground piquín chile

Finely grated fresh coconut or unsweetened flaked coconut

## TEXTURE

A luxuriant "mouth feel" happens to be one of the first things novices can detect when they begin tasting chocolate. "*So smooth!*" people will say with approval at tastings. Yes, this can be a pleasurable effect and a mark of excellence when combined with great flavor—but don't let the presence or absence of a satiny texture distract you from the real business of identifying flavors. I tend to think about texture only after I feel I've done justice to the actual flavors. Some chocolates are unbelievably smooth and creamy, some just a little gritty. We are often told of the Swiss preference for a super-smooth texture, achieved by conching for days on end. But conching chocolate beyond a certain degree is really meaningless, since any breakdown of the particles during refining to a size smaller than eighteen microns is indiscernible to the palate. In addition, overconching can increase the viscosity of a chocolate through evaporation, causing an overall loss of flavor.

## Appreciating and Choosing Chocolate

*When you work with chocolate every day, mediocrity is abhorred.*

BILL YOSSES,
PASTRY CHEF, NEW YORK CITY

Which chocolate to choose must always depend on your purpose: fine desserts or truffles, ganaches and sauces, hot chocolate, decorative molding, or artistic chocolate shapes. It is also a matter of personal preference—but I believe that preference has to be informed by knowledge.

Your first step must be learning to read labels. Chocolate makers are increasingly aware that people want to know what is in their chocolate. Not all labels are ideally informative, but several companies are starting to provide data on some crucial matters. The most important facts, besides the origin of the beans, are total cacao content and cacao butter content. Standards vary widely, but in this country only chocolates with more than 35 percent cacao content can be labeled bittersweet chocolate or couverture (the French require only a minimum of 32 percent cacao content).

The point is important because cacao content is what makes chocolate taste like chocolate, no matter what its intended purpose. Standard supermarket candy bars typically have extremely low cacao content (perhaps only the legal minimum of 15 percent for a milk chocolate) and are beefed up with fillers and sugar. Good eating bittersweet chocolates will have at least the basic 35 percent cacao content. Premium chocolates (for both eating and cooking) will usually have much more, from 41 percent for a first-class milk chocolate to 70 or 75 percent cacao content for an especially intense dark chocolate.

Chocolate for decorative purposes may be another case. Because cacao butter is expensive and can be difficult to work with, special compound chocolates have been devised with partly hydrogenated fats that require no tempering and that mimic the qualities of cacao butter. However, they are invariably inferior from a flavor standpoint.

The only way to familiarize yourself with the range of possibilities is to buy and taste different chocolates, taking into account the amount of cacao listed. You can begin by looking at what is available in stores near you, even supermarkets. If the cacao content is not on the label, call the company and ask for the information. You will soon learn to recognize the different intensities. You will also start sensing the difference between synthetic and real vanilla.

It would be easy to think that the best chocolate is the one with the highest cacao content, but it is not that simple. You must take into account factors such as the original beans and the handling they have received, as well as your intended purpose. For example, if you are making hot chocolate, the richest product available may yield a disappointing result with an unsightly film of melted fat on top. This is the result of extra cacao butter added to some premium chocolates to decrease viscosity. The same too-rich chocolate might be perfect for "enrobing" (coating) truffles, where smoothness and fluidity are everything. A not-so-smooth industrial chocolate with great flavor and no added cacao butter might be great for hot chocolate. Even better are the grainy, powdery-looking, wonderfully spiced artisanal Latin American cacao balls.

The couverture-quality chocolates used in these recipes are also ideal eating chocolates. I consider them to be among the finest fruits of human art and science. What lifts a chocolate into the realm of the superlative? It is a matter of noble flavor beans in the hands of the right people making the right choices as they oversee a battery of powerful, sophisticated machinery from five-roller mills to open conches. Skilled chocolatiers must judge the chemical and physical attributes of the cacao liquor as it is transformed from a gritty mass into something ineffably silky, fragrant, and tantalizing. For me an exceptional couverture is one that seamlessly blends complex flavor and aroma together with full, velvety mouth feel.

My idea of the ultimate chocolate dessert—and the ultimate education in the subtleties of chocolate—is a large sampling platter with at least a dozen chocolates made by different manufacturers and representing a wide gamut of flavors, textures, and cacao contents. It's a wonderful way to hone your tasting skills with company.

# Recipes

The following recipes have one quality in common: they showcase the wide-ranging possibilities of chocolate and imaginatively explore its capacity to absorb flavors and harmonize with other flavorings and spices.

They are culled from contemporary chefs who have learned how to work with a new generation of high cacao–content chocolates, and from traditional Latin American cooks who know cacao intimately. The chefs build their recipes around particular brands of chocolate, drawing on their distinctive characters and cacao contents to create subtle variations of flavor and aroma. They use chocolate as they would a spice, highlighting its nuances and pairing it with a spectrum of exciting flavorings. This approach is, of course, nothing new; it was practiced by colonial cooks, and it can be traced back to the Maya and Aztecs.

These recipes range from the modest and simple to the grand and complex. There are traditional Latin American recipes such as homemade cacao balls, which are grated and used to make hot chocolate, and modern creations such as Harold McGee's unusual cheese and chocolate truffles. There are classics such as the Viennese Sachertorte, and playful new inventions such as chocolate soup. There are also recipes from the sixteenth and seventeenth centuries, whose sophisticated blend of spices can inspire the contemporary chef.

Don't think of these recipes as culinary straitjackets. Though each recipe calls for particular brands of chocolate with specific percentages of cacao content, substitutions are always possible. Given the range of chocolates available today, cooks have more choices than ever before.

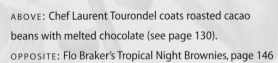

ABOVE: Chef Laurent Tourondel coats roasted cacao beans with melted chocolate (see page 130).
OPPOSITE: Flo Braker's Tropical Night Brownies, page 146

# Laurent Tourondel's Two-Toned Candied Cacao Beans Dipped in Chocolate

*At Laurent Tourondel's Manhattan restaurant Cello, this diverting invention is offered in small, elegant, silver-lidded wooden boxes along with coffee and desserts. It's a prime example of how chocolate is being explored by a new generation of chefs who value cacao in its own right, as well as in different manufactured forms. Here is a triple treat: nutty beans with a rich chocolate coating and final dusting of cocoa.*

**• MAKES ABOUT 4 CUPS (2 CUPS OF EACH COLOR)**

2 cups granulated sugar

³/₄ cup water

12 ounces (about 3 cups) whole unroasted cacao beans

10 ounces El Rey Gran Samán dark chocolate (70% cacao) or Valrhona Guanaja dark chocolate (70% cacao)

1 cup Valrhona or other cocoa powder

1 cup sifted confectioners' sugar

Dissolve the sugar in the water in a heavy 4-quart saucepan. Over high heat, cook the syrup to 310°F, or slightly below the light caramel stage (it should be just starting to color a little). Remove the pan from the heat at once and start adding the cacao beans, stirring them rapidly with a wooden spoon. Quickly return the pan to high heat and keep stirring furiously to coat them all over with the syrup. This will coat the beans with a delicious crunchy armor, as well as roast them.

Pour out the mass onto a baking sheet. The beans will crackle and the sugar will begin to crystallize. As soon as it is cool enough to handle, break it apart into separate beans embedded in crystallized lumps of pale tan sugar. Slide the baking sheet into the freezer and chill for 20 to 30 minutes.

While the coated beans are chilling, break the chocolate into 8 to 10 pieces and place in the top of a double boiler or heatproof bowl over simmering water. Heat until evenly melted. Remove from the heat and work with a rubber spatula to keep the chocolate smooth while it cools slightly. It should be just above room temperature but still liquid.

Remove the sugared beans from the freezer and pour into a large mixing bowl. Drizzle with about half the melted chocolate and turn the beans with the rubber spatula to start coating them. Add the remaining chocolate; stir and toss with the spatula to distribute the chocolate evenly over the beans before it hardens too much to work. Again separate the mass into individual coated beans. Place them on a baking sheet and chill in the freezer for 3 to 4 minutes.

Spread the cocoa powder over a large deep plate and the confectioners' sugar over another. Remove the chocolate-coated beans from the freezer. Gently roll half the beans in the cocoa, half in the sugar (it is best to work with a small amount at a time).

Line a tray or baking sheet with waxed paper. With a wire skimmer or slotted spoon, lift out the beans a few at a time, shaking off excess cocoa or sugar, and place on the waxed paper.

To serve, arrange the different-colored beans in alternating rows in a small candy dish or individual dishes. Allow for 4 per person unless there is a stampede for more.

*Note:* Chef Tourondel suggests storing the white and brown beans in separate airtight containers, packed in additional cocoa or confectioners' sugar. They will keep in the refrigerator for 2 to 3 months.

# Harold McGee's Chocolate-Cheese Truffles

*Harold McGee, the author of* On Food and Cooking, *is my guru for all kinds of food chemistry questions. He tells me that a few years ago he heard that a celebrated Parisian chocolatier was making cheese-filled chocolates. Harold was intrigued by the combination because chocolate and cheese both go through fermentation stages that produce a number of flavor notes in common—a potential bridge between two otherwise highly contrasting foods. When he eventually got to sample the chocolates in question, he was less than enchanted by the way the idea had been realized. However, his disappointment only spurred him to experiment and create the following new twist on truffles.*

*McGee finds that of the three suggested chocolate-cheese pairings, the Camembert provides "a buttery richness, the goat cheese a creamy piquancy, the blue cheese a savory saltiness." (Do not try Roquefort instead of the Stilton or Gorgonzola; it will be too salty and sharp.) Serve the truffles at the end of a meal with a complex red wine like a Banyuls or late-harvest Zinfandel.*

• MAKES **12** TO **18** TRUFFLES

**FILLING**
4 ounces (weight without rind) ripe
    Camembert, fresh goat's milk cheese, or
    Stilton or Gorgonzola, at room temperature

1 tablespoon superfine sugar

1 to 2 ounces Scharffen Berger dark chocolate
    (70% cacao), finely chopped

**COATING**
6 ounces Scharffen Berger dark chocolate (70%
    cacao), finely chopped

Trim any rind from the cheese and bring it to room temperature. In a mixing bowl, combine the cheese and sugar and mix until the sugar has dissolved.

Melt the filling chocolate in the top of a double boiler over simmering water. Use 1 ounce chocolate for Camembert and goat cheese fillings; use 2 ounces for blue cheese fillings. Make sure the cheese you use is at room temperature and very soft. If it is too firm, microwave it very briefly to soften it.

Combine the melted chocolate, superfine sugar, and cheese and work together with a wooden spoon or flexible spatula until the mixture is homogeneous. (This may be easier if you add a few drops of water or a little butter.) If the mixture is too soft to shape, refrigerate for 15 to 20 minutes.

Roll portions of the mixture into $^{1}/_{2}$-inch balls and refrigerate for 15 to 20 minutes. Melt and temper the coating chocolate according to the directions on pages 134 and 135. Dip the cheese balls in the tempered chocolate, letting the excess drain off. Allow to set at room temperature. Keep in a cool place and serve on the same day.

*Note:* Cheese will resume fermentation if left at room temperature, so this is one case where truffles should be refrigerated if kept for more than a day. Place on a sheet or tray and wrap snugly in waxed paper, then plastic wrap, before refrigerating. Allow to warm to room temperature before unwrapping.

## HOW TO TEMPER CHOCOLATE

To coat truffles or molded candies evenly and attractively with melted chocolate, you must outwit the natural tendency of the cacao butter to separate into several different crystal forms when warmed above and then cooled below some critical temperature points. There are different strategies one can take to temper chocolate—that is, to stabilize the cacao butter into one uniform kind of crystal configuration that will not cause the chocolate to discolor or be grainy when it hardens after melting. The seemingly simplest techniques actually require a great deal of familiarity with chocolate.

### The "Mush" Method

Veteran California chocolate technologist Terry Richardson—a respected teacher and consultant to the chocolate industry—has developed a foolproof method of tempering that produces chocolate with a high gloss. He calls it the "mush" method. I have slightly modified it for amateurs who are dedicated enough to carry out a precise scenario.

You must be organized and preferably have a couple of double boilers at the ready along with one quick-reading chocolate thermometer that can register fine differences between 65° and 150°F. You will need a clean, nonporous work surface (marble, polished granite, stainless steel, or Formica), a spatula with a thin flexible blade, and a small electric fan or a hair dryer set on cool.

This method is particularly useful for dark chocolate couvertures with 100 percent cacao butter and for chocolates aged for over three months. Milk chocolate requires a different temperature range. (Richardson emphasizes the importance of contacting manufacturers for precise instructions on tempering their milk chocolates, since dairy butterfat content varies widely.)

1. Finely chop the chocolate (any amount) and place it in the top of a double boiler or in a a metal or heatproof glass bowl nested in another bowl filled halfway with simmering water. Melt and heat the chocolate until it is between 120° and 130°F. (Richardson goes as high as 140°F, to ensure that all of the fat crystals are properly melted.)

2. Have ready another double-boiler bottom (or similar-sized pan) filled halfway with water at about 70°F; place the melted chocolate over this, off the heat, occasionally stirring gently, until the chocolate cools to about 94°F. Be careful not to create air pockets during the cooling and stirring.

3. When the chocolate reaches about 94°F, place the bowl over the first double-boiler bottom (the water in the double boiler should be about 94° to 95°F by now). Pour about one-fifth of the chocolate onto a clean work surface. Quickly start "mushing" the chocolate on the work surface by scraping it back and forth with a thin flexible spatula. When the "mush" acquires a dull and mattelike surface (about 8 minutes), scrape it off the board back into the rest of the chocolate in the double-boiler top. Stir in the mush until completely blended into the rest of the chocolate; the temperature of the chocolate after blending should be between 89° and 91°F.

4. Check the tempering by cooling a small sample of the chocolate on a piece of aluminum foil in front of an electric fan or a hair dryer on a cool setting. The chocolate should set relatively quickly and be glossy and smooth, not dull. It is now ready for dipping. If the chocolate becomes too thick for dipping after a while, add some warm chocolate that has been melted until it is between 120° and 130°F, cooled, and kept warm at 89°F to 91F°. Be careful not to let the temperature of the tempered choco-

late rise above 91°F; if it gets too warm, the chocolate might lose its temper.

5. If the chocolate does overheat, retemper as follows: grate a very small amount (2% of the weight of the melted dipping chocolate will be enough) from a tempered bar or block on the fine side of a box grater. Add the grated chocolate to the dipping chocolate and mix until the mass is free of lumps.

For best results, it is important that you cool your dipped chocolate under a fan in a room at a temperature between 70° and 75°F.

## The Seed Method

This popular method consists of heating the chocolate to the point at which all crystal forms are melted and cooling it by adding a small amount of reserved unmelted chocolate. Because the reserved chocolate has not gone "out of temper" through heating, it will "seed" the cacao butter with stable crystals.

1. Weigh the amount of chocolate called for in the recipe, and set aside a chunk that is about 10% of the total weight. Finely chop the larger amount; grate the remaining chunk on the fine side of a box grater.

2. Place the chopped chocolate in the top of a double boiler or in a clean, dry, stainless steel bowl set over a pot filled halfway with simmering water. Allow the chocolate to begin melting at 120°F. (Chocolate technologist Terry Richardson recommends temperatures between 130° and 140°F for dark chocolates with high cacao content that have been aged for over three months). Then remove it from the heat. Have ready another double-boiler bottom (or similar-sized pan) filled halfway with water at about 70°F. Place the bowl of melted chocolate over this, off the heat, and let sit, occa-

sionally stirring gently, until the chocolate cools to 94°F. Be careful not to create air pockets during the cooling and stirring.

3. Add the reserved unmelted grated chocolate and stir with a wooden spoon until all the chocolate has melted, all lumps are gone, and the temperature has cooled to between 89°F and 91°F. To test the degree of tempering, cool a small sample of the chocolate on a piece of aluminum foil in front of an electric fan or a hair dryer on a cool setting. The chocolate should be glossy and smooth. Keep the chocolate in the double boiler over warm water (about 94°F) while you are dipping. Do not allow the temperature of the dark chocolate to rise above 91°F; if it gets too warm, the chocolate may lose its temper. If the chocolate becomes too thick for dipping or loses its temper, follow the instructions in Step 5 of the "mush" method.

## Jim Graham's Quick Seed Method

Chicago-based master chocolatier and industry consultant Jim Graham has devised a quick and painless seed tempering method for the home cook. It is very similar to the seed method, but in place of Step 1, dark chocolate should be finely chopped and 10 percent of the total weight set aside. Follow Step 2 of the procedure, heating the chocolate to 120°F and cooling it to 94°F. Transfer it to a tall, narrow container. Add the reserved chocolate. Place a handheld immersion blender in the chocolate to submerge the blades completely and turn to high speed, moving the blender in the chocolate with a stirring motion. A variable-speed blender will allow you to reduce the speed if the friction of the blades starts to overheat the chocolate. To test the degree of tempering and for retempering instructions, see Steps 4 and 5 of the "mush" method.

# Fran Bigelow's Deep Chocolate Torte

*Fran Bigelow is the grand dame of American chocolate confection, and her shop in Seattle is a mecca for chocolate afficionados. She is famous for deluxe versions of popular standbys, like candy bars, made with pure Venezuelan chocolate and enhanced with cacao nibs, coffee beans, and candied orange peel. She also has a reputation for using the best sweet ingredients and delivering the deepest chocolate flavor—as in this rich flourless torte, which is a cross between an eggy pudding and a nonpuffy soufflé.*

• MAKES ONE **9**-INCH TORTE (ABOUT **8** SERVINGS)

**1 pound dark chocolate, preferably Cacao Barry Equateur (60% cacao) or Callebaut (56% cacao), finely chopped**

**6 eggs**

**¹/₄ cup sugar**

**2 tablespoons Grand Marnier or other liqueur**

**1 cup heavy cream**

**Cocoa for dusting**

Place the chocolate in a heatproof bowl or the top of a double boiler over barely simmering water and allow to melt completely.

Preheat the oven to 350°F. Generously butter a 9-inch round regular or springform cake pan. Cut a 9-inch round of waxed paper and press it over the bottom of the pan.

Beat the eggs, sugar, and liqueur in a large heatproof mixing bowl. Place the bowl over a saucepan of simmering water, stirring with a wooden spoon, until warm but not hot. Remove from the heat and transfer to the bowl of an electric mixer. Beat with the whisk attachment for 5 minutes. Slowly stir in the melted chocolate.

Whip the cream to soft peaks and gently fold into the chocolate mixture. Carefully transfer the batter to the pan.

Bake for 40 minutes, or until a straw or cake tester inserted into the torte at least 2 to 4 inches from the side comes out clean. The center should be just set; do not overbake.

Let cool to room temperature, remove from the pan, and peel off the liner. It is best served with a simple dusting of cocoa; accompaniments like unsweetened whipped cream or raspberry sauce are optional. If necessary, you can refrigerate the torte for up to 1 day, covered with plastic wrap, but bring to room temperature before serving.

# Bill Yosses's Soft Chocolate Cake with Banana-Raisin Sauce and Lime Cream

*Rich, moist, all-but-flourless chocolate cakes are now almost standard in the modern patisserie. This version developed by Bill Yosses, formerly the pastry chef at New York's Bouley Bakery and now the executive pastry chef at Citarella's shops and restaurant, has especially clean, well-defined flavors rather than an overwhelming mélange of effects. For the chocolate, Bill prefers Valrhona Manjari or Pur Caraïbe; other possible choices are Callebaut bittersweet or Lindt Excellence. He likes to serve the cake with Champagne, a sweet moscato, or Sauternes (Bill's in-your-dreams suggestion is a 1945 Chateau D'Yquem!).*

• MAKES **6** SERVINGS

## CAKE

8 ounces dark chocolate, such as Valrhona Manjari (64% cacao) or Valrhona Pur Caraïbe (66% cacao), chopped into quarter-sized pieces

1 cup (2 sticks) unsalted butter, cut into cubes

4 eggs

1¹/₂ cups sugar

¹/₂ cup all-purpose flour

## GARNISH

¹/₄ cup water

¹/₄ teaspoon ground cinnamon or 2 blackberry or mint tea bags

¹/₄ cup golden raisins

2 ripe bananas

1 tablespoon dark rum

1 tablespoon granulated sugar

Juice and grated zest of 1 lime

¹/₂ cup heavy cream

2 tablespoons confectioners' sugar

To make the cake, preheat the oven to 350°F. Line a well-buttered 10-inch round cake pan with a 10-inch circle of parchment paper.

Place the chopped chocolate and butter in the top of a double boiler or heatproof bowl over boiling water. Remove from the heat and let it sit until melted, stirring occasionally. Keep warm, off the heat, while you work.

Whisk the eggs and sugar together in a mixing bowl until light and foamy, about 3 minutes. Sift the flour over the mixture, whisking to incorporate smoothly. With a rubber spatula, fold the batter into the warm chocolate mixture.

Pour the batter into the prepared pan and bake for 35 minutes. Let the cake cool in the pan for about 30 minutes.

Have ready a serving plate or platter an inch or two larger than the cake pan. Place it firmly over the top and invert the cake onto the platter, tapping it firmly to help loosen it. Peel off the parchment layer. Let sit at room temperature until you are ready to serve.

To prepare the garnish, first make the raisin-banana sauce. Heat the water in a small pan with the cinnamon or tea bags. When it comes to a boil, stir in the raisins and set aside to cool. Peel the bananas and cut into $1/4$-inch slices.

Combine the rum and the sugar in a sauté pan over medium heat and add the lime juice, reserving the grated zest. When the sugar melts, add the bananas and cook over low heat for 3 to 4 minutes, gently turning to coat the

pieces evenly. Set aside in the pan until you are ready to serve.

Whip the cream with 1 tablespoon of the confectioners' sugar; when it forms stiff peaks, fold in the reserved lime zest. Refrigerate until you are ready to serve.

At serving time, combine the raisin and banana mixtures in the sauté pan and reheat to boiling. Cut the cake into 6 wedges with a long sharp knife, wiping the blade clean after each cut. Place each piece on a serving plate and spoon some of the hot banana-raisin mixture next to it. With a soup spoon dipped in hot water, spoon some of the lime-flavored whipped cream over each piece. Sift a little of the remaining 1 tablespoon confectioners' sugar over each portion and serve.

# Elizabeth Falkner's Scharffen Berger Roulade

*This jelly roll for grown-ups comes from the irrepressible Elizabeth Falkner, a former film-student-turned-pâtissière who makes show-stopping desserts at her pastry shop and cafe, Citizen Cake, in San Francisco. Elizabeth fills a delicate textured chocolate sponge with an Earl Grey tea–infused ganache and orange marmalade, then repeats the Earl Grey accent in the whipped cream. Elizabeth recommends using a quality tea with a fine bergamot fragrance. The secret to the cake is the rice flour, which adds a subtle crunch to the texture. You can find it in natural foods stores and Asian markets.*

• SERVES **8**

### GANACHE FILLING

8 ounces Scharffen Berger dark chocolate (70% cacao), finely chopped

1 cup heavy cream

2 tablespoons corn syrup

1 tablespoon loose Earl Grey tea leaves

### EARL GREY WHIPPED CREAM

2 cups heavy cream

2 tablespoons sugar

2 teaspoons loose Earl Grey tea leaves

### CAKE

$^1/_2$ cup nonalkalized cocoa powder

$^1/_2$ cup Guistos or other sweet rice flour

$^1/_4$ teaspoon baking soda (omit if using Dutch alkalized cocoa powder)

4 eggs, separated

$^1/_3$ cup plus $^3/_4$ cup sugar

$^1/_2$ cup cold water

$^1/_2$ teaspoon cream of tartar

$^1/_2$ teaspoon salt

Confectioners' sugar for dusting

1 cup bitter (Seville) orange marmalade

To make the ganache filling, place the chopped chocolate in a small mixing bowl and set aside. Combine the cream, corn syrup, and tea in a nonreactive saucepan and bring just to a boil over medium-high heat. Remove from the heat and let steep for 15 minutes. Return to a simmer, then immediately pour the mixture through a fine-mesh strainer into the bowl of chocolate. Press with a spoon to extract as much liquid as possible from the tea leaves.

Whisk to melt the chocolate into the steeped cream. Pour into a shallow container and cover the surface with plastic wrap. Refrigerate overnight. Let sit at room temperature for 2 to 3 hours before using.

To steep the cream for whipping, place 1 cup of the cream, the sugar, and tea in a small saucepan. Bring just to a boil; remove from the heat and let steep for 15 minutes. Strain through a fine-mesh strainer. Add the remaining cup of cream. Refrigerate until very cold, at least 3 hours.

To make the cake, preheat the oven to 350°F. Coat a 17 x 12-inch sheet cake pan with shortening or spray with nonstick oil. Line the bottom of the pan with parchment paper and coat lightly with shortening or oil. Dust the surface with flour and tap out the excess.

Sift the cocoa, rice flour, and baking soda (if using) into a small mixing bowl and set aside. In a large mixing bowl, whisk the egg yolks together with the $^1/_3$ cup of sugar, vigorously whipping until they are pale yellow in color, about 45 seconds. Add the water and stir until smooth. Add the sifted cocoa mixture and whisk until smooth.

In the clean bowl of a mixer fitted with the wire whip attachment, whip the egg whites, cream of tartar, and salt until foamy, about 30 seconds. Increase the speed to medium-high and slowly add the $^3/_4$ cup sugar, beating until the whites are glossy and hold stiff peaks, about 2 minutes.

Spoon about one-quarter of the whites into the bowl with the chocolate mixture. With a whisk, stir the whites into the chocolate mixture to lighten it. Using a rubber spatula, fold in the remaining whites, folding just until no streaks remain.

Pour the batter into the prepared pan. Using an offset spatula, quickly smooth the surface. Bake for 10 to 12 minutes, until the edges start to pull away from the sides of the pan and the surface is dry and doesn't stick to your fingertip when lightly touched.

Have ready a piece of parchment paper. Remove the cake from the oven and cool in the pan on a rack for 5 minutes. Run a small knife along the perimeter of the pan to loosen the cake. Sift the confectioners' sugar over the surface of the cake. Cover with the parchment. Invert the cake onto the work surface, being careful not to dislodge the parchment. Gently peel away the parchment. Let the cake cool.

To fill the cake, soften the room-temperature ganache to a spreadable consistency by beating it with the whisk attachment until smooth, lighter in color, and increased in volume, about 45 seconds. Dot the marmalade evenly over the surface of the cooled cake. Gently spread the marmalade evenly over the cake with an icing spatula. Spread the ganache over the layer of marmalade.

Starting with a short end, gently fold over 2 inches of the cake. Carefully peel off the sugar-dusted parchment. Continue to roll the cake, using the parchment to lift and roll it. Wrap the cake in plastic wrap, and place seam side down on a tray. Chill for at least 2 hours.

To serve, unwrap the roulade and bring to room temperature. Whip the cream to soft peaks. Dust the cake with confectioners' sugar. With a serrated knife dipped in hot water, cut the cake into 1-inch slices, wiping the knife clean between cuts. Spoon a dollop of the whipped cream over each slice.

# Wayne Brachman's Pecan–Guaranda Chocolate Tart with Mango and Papaya

*Wayne Harley Brachman, a cookbook author and the executive pastry chef for the Glacier group restaurants in New York, has come up with an innovative refinement on old-fashioned pecan pie. His version features tropical fruits, a crackly caramel finish, and the flavorful Chocovic Guaranda chocolate (made near Barcelona from Ecuadorian beans), which he uses to make a luxurious ganache that is spread over the pecan filling.*

• MAKES ONE 9$^{1}$/$_{2}$-INCH TART

## TART SHELL

1$^{1}$/$_{2}$ cups all-purpose flour

1 tablespoon sugar

$^{1}$/$_{2}$ cup (1 stick) cold unsalted butter, cut into pea-sized bits

1 egg, lightly beaten with $^{1}$/$_{2}$ cup ice water

## FILLING

$^{3}$/$_{4}$ cup sugar, plus 3 tablespoons for glaze

4 eggs

1 cup dark corn syrup

2 tablespoons dark rum

1 tablespoon pure vanilla extract

4 tablespoons ($^{1}$/$_{2}$ stick) unsalted butter, melted

2 cups (10 ounces) pecan halves

4 ounces Chocovic Guaranda dark chocolate (71% cacao), finely chopped

$^{1}$/$_{2}$ cup heavy cream

1 small ripe papaya, peeled, seeded, and cut into $^{1}$/$_{2}$-inch dice

1 ripe mango, peeled, seeded, and diced

To make the tart shell, stir together the flour and sugar in a large mixing bowl. With an electric mixer, your fingertips, or a pastry blender, work the butter into the mixture until it resembles coarse meal. Sprinkle 3 to 4 tablespoons of the egg–ice water mixture over the mixture and mix it in until the dough comes together in a ball. Shape the dough into a disk, wrap in plastic, and refrigerate overnight or for at least 2 hours.

Lightly coat the removable bottom of a 9$^{1}$/$_{2}$-inch tart pan with nonstick vegetable oil spray. On a lightly floured surface, roll out the dough into an 11$^{1}$/$_{2}$-inch circle. Fit the dough into the pan and trim to an even 1-inch overhang. Fold over the excess on itself to reinforce the edges; press and pinch into a fluted wall. Refrigerate for 20 minutes.

Preheat the oven to 400°F. Line the inner surface of the pastry with aluminum foil and weight down with dried beans or pie weights.

Bake on the center rack of the oven for 15 minutes. Lift out the foil with the beans or weights; bake for 8 minutes longer, or until just lightly browned. Cool to room temperature on a rack.

When you are ready to assemble the tart, preheat the oven to 325°F.

In a large mixing bowl, combine ³/₄ cup of the sugar with the eggs, corn syrup, rum, and vanilla extract. Mix well and beat in the melted butter.

Spread the pecans evenly across the tart shell. Carefully pour the sugar-egg mixture over the pecans, making sure that the nuts are covered and no filling has dripped over the pastry. Bake for 30 minutes, until you see bubbles appearing around the edges of the filling. Cool to room temperature on a rack.

To make the ganache topping, place the chocolate in a small bowl and set aside. Bring the cream to a boil in a small saucepan over medium heat. Remove from the heat at once and pour the cream over the chocolate. Working from the center out, gently stir with a whisk to melt and blend. Keep stirring until smooth. Spread the mixture evenly over the top of the baked and filled tart. Cool until set.

Arrange the fruit over the tart and refrigerate for 15 minutes. Sprinkle the remaining 3 tablespoons of sugar evenly over the fruit and caramelize with a propane torch or by placing briefly under a preheated broiler. Slice into wedges and serve.

# Markus Farbinger's Classic Sachertorte

Markus Farbinger is a former dean of the baking and pastry curriculum at the Culinary Institute of America at Hyde Park, and now you can find him doing something he loves as much as teaching— making beautiful chocolate at Larry Burdick's shop in Walpole, New Hampshire, where he is a managing partner. His roots are solidly Austrian: he grew up working at his parents' fourth-generation bread bakery in the mountain village of Taxenbach, and his experience in his native country includes a stint at the Hotel Sacher in Vienna, the first and only true home of the famous Sachertorte.

Unlike some takeoffs that borrow the Sacher name, Farbinger's recipe has the classic simplicity of the original. It is very close to an old-fashioned pound cake, but spongier and drier. Farbinger loves Sachertorte with a generous dollop of very lightly sweetened, vanilla-flavored whipped cream on the side. (Purists, he acknowledges, frown on such embellishments.) If possible, follow the weight measurements as given by Farbinger for the truest replication of his recipe.

More difficult to make than the cake itself, the fondant-type icing is a sine qua non *for a true Sachertorte. It should have an almost mirrorlike sheen. You will need a clean nonporous work surface (marble is best; otherwise polished granite, stainless steel, or Formica). Be sure to work in a draft-free room. Warm the work surface by placing a bowl of hot water on it; remove when you are ready to work the glaze with a spatula. Have ready a quick-reading thermometer and a small pastry brush dipped in water.*

• MAKES ONE **10**-INCH CAKE

## TORTE

4³/₄ ounces dark chocolate, preferably Valrhona Pur Caraibe (66% cacao), finely chopped

9 tablespoons (1 stick plus 1 tablespoon, 4³/₄ ounces) unsalted butter

1 cup plus 2 tablespoons (4 ounces) confectioners' sugar

6 eggs, separated

1 cup plus 2 tablespoons (4 ounces) granulated sugar

1 cup (4¹/₂ ounces) all-purpose flour

1 cup (8 ounces) apricot jam, preferably Darbo brand (available at pastry-supply shops)

## SACHER CHOCOLATE GLAZE

1 cup (7 ounces) granulated sugar

3 tablespoons water

6 ounces dark chocolate, preferably El Rey Gran Samán (70% cacao), finely chopped

## VANILLA-SCENTED WHIPPED CREAM

1 cup heavy cream

2 tablespoons granulated sugar

1 teaspoon pure vanilla extract

In the top of a double boiler, melt the chocolate over simmering water. Set aside.

Preheat the oven to 350°F. Butter and flour a 10-inch round cake pan with 2-inch-high sides.

In the mixing bowl of a standing mixer fitted with the wire whisk attachment, cream the butter with the confectioners' sugar. Beat in the melted chocolate. Add the egg yolks one at a time. Scrape down the sides of the bowl as necessary.

In a separate bowl, beat the egg whites until foamy. Gradually add the granulated sugar, beating continuously until the mixture forms glossy, moderately firm peaks. Gently fold the egg whites into the butter-chocolate mixture. Fold in the flour gently but completely.

Pour the batter into the cake pan and level the surface with a spatula. Bake for 70 minutes. Cool slightly in the pan, then turn out onto a cloth and cool completely, upside down.

With a long, thin knife, slice the cake horizontally into two thin layers. Spread about half of the apricot jam over the bottom layer. Replace the top layer, warm the rest of the jam, and spread it evenly over the top. Let stand until the jam has cooled enough to lose its shininess and looks slightly congealed.

To make the glaze, in a small heavy saucepan, bring the sugar and water to a boil over medium heat and add the chocolate. Heat to 250°F, frequently washing down the sides of the pan with a wet pastry brush. When the mixture is 250°F, a small amount dropped from a spoon will form a thin thread.

Remove the pan from the heat. Pour a small amount of the glaze onto a nonporous surface (preferably marble) and quickly work it with a pastry knife until it begins to look a little pale and opaque. Immediately scrape it back into the pan and stir to combine with the rest. Repeat the process, each time working a little of the mixture until it looks light and milky and quickly recombining with the rest. Do not overwork. When the glaze is ready, it will have good body but still be fluid; the temperature should be about 80°F.

To ice the torte, slowly pour the glaze over it, evenly covering the top and sides with a few strokes of an icing spatula. Immediately lift the cake off the rack and onto a baking sheet or serving plate and let stand until the icing is thoroughly set, at least 2 hours.

In a chilled mixing bowl, whip the cream, sugar, and vanilla just until the mixture holds soft peaks.

To serve, cut the torte with a knife dipped in water and wiped clean before each new cut. Add a dollop of whipped cream, if desired. The torte should never be refrigerated. It will last 2 to 3 days at room temperature.

# Flo Braker's Tropical Night Brownies

*My favorite photograph of the Venezuelan tours on which I introduced chefs and food writers to the home territory of chocolate shows cookbook author Flo Braker joyously coated in glistening chocolate from stem to stern like a swamp creature emerging from a mud bath. Another memory I cherish is of a wondrous tropical night at the secluded beach of Playa Medina in the Paria Peninsula and Flo making brownies in the humble kitchen of our hotel, with waves lapping almost to the doorstep and the mingled aromas of salt sea and Venezuelan chocolate filling the tropical night. She used just the ingredients that we could get our hands on there, including fresh coconut, cashews, Venezuelan rum, the local brown loaf sugar (papelón), and of course cacao nibs and chocolate. Here is Flo's re-creation of that memorable recipe.*

• MAKES **16** BROWNIES

10 tablespoons (1¼ sticks) **unsalted butter**

2 ounces **El Rey Gran Samán dark chocolate (70% cacao) or Scharffen Berger dark chocolate (70% cacao), finely chopped**

3 ounces **El Rey Bucare dark chocolate (58.5% cacao), finely chopped**

1 cup packed **light brown sugar**

½ cup **granulated sugar**

3 **eggs**, lightly beaten

1 tablespoon **dark rum**

1 teaspoon **pure vanilla extract**

½ cup plus 1 tablespoon unsifted **all-purpose flour**

¼ teaspoon **salt**

¼ cup **unsweetened medium flaked coconut** or 1 cup **fresh coconut**, grated on the medium side of a box grater

½ cup (1½ ounces) **unsalted roasted cashews**, coarsely chopped

¼ cup finely chopped **cacao nibs**

Place a rack in the lower third of the oven and preheat to 350°F.

In a small saucepan over low heat, melt the butter with the chocolate. Remove from the heat and stir in both sugars. Pour into a large mixing bowl and set aside to cool for about 5 minutes.

Add the eggs, rum, and vanilla, stirring just until blended. Stir in the flour and salt, then the coconut, cashews, and cacao nibs.

Spread the batter in a greased 9 x 9-inch baking pan. Bake for 22 minutes. Cool thoroughly before cutting into 16 squares, each about 2¼ x 2¼ inches.

# Chocolate Jasmine Ice Cream

*In a much-celebrated Italian recipe from the Renaissance, created in honor of the Duke of Tuscany, alternating layers of fresh jasmine blossoms and crushed cacao nibs were allowed to sit for 24 hours until the flavors were fused. This is a lovely idea—cacao and chocolate, with their high fat content, are known for an amazing capacity to absorb taste and fragrance. I've adopted the same combination for another purpose, a smooth and creamy ice cream based on Venezuelan milk chocolate and jasmine tea. To me this is an all-time magical union of tropical perfumes. It deserves to become a classic.*

• MAKES ABOUT 5¹/₂ CUPS

3¹/₂ cups fresh whole milk

1 vanilla bean, preferably Mexican, split lengthwise, seeds scraped and reserved

¹/₈ teaspoon salt

¹/₂ cup loose jasmine tea leaves

¹/₂ cup heavy cream

6 egg yolks

1 cup dark brown sugar, preferably finely grated piloncillo or panela (Latin brown loaf sugar) or dark muscovado or Demerara natural cane sugar

7 ounces El Rey Caoba milk chocolate (41% cacao) or Valrhona Jivara milk chocolate (40% cacao), finely chopped

In a 3-quart heavy-bottomed saucepan, heat the milk, the vanilla bean, scraped seeds, and salt. Bring to a boil, reduce the heat to low, add the jasmine tea, simmer for 2 to 3 minutes, and remove from the heat. Allow the mixture to stand for 15 minutes, to steep the tea in the cream. When the cream mixture has cooled, strain through a fine-mesh strainer into a spouted container. Using the back of a spoon, press the tea leaves to remove as much of the liquid as possible. Rinse and dry the pot.

To make the ice cream custard, beat the egg yolks with the brown sugar until thick and fluffy, about 5 minutes, using a standing mixer or a hand mixer. Reduce the speed to low and pour the cream mixture gradually into the egg mixture while beating. Pour the mixture back into the pot and simmer, stirring, over very low heat until it thickens and coats the back of the spoon, about 4 to 5 minutes.

Place the chopped chocolate in a bowl and pour the hot custard over it. Allow it to stand for 1 minute, then mix it thoroughly with a spatula until smooth and creamy. Strain through a fine-mesh strainer into a bowl. Set the bowl in a larger bowl filled with cracked ice and water to cool the custard, stirring often.

When the custard is at room temperature, pour into the bowl of an ice cream maker and process according to the manufacturer's instructions until fully frozen. Scoop into a stainless steel or plastic container and place in the freezer to harden for 2 to 4 hours for optimum texture.

*Note:* An important ingredient is the richly flavored unrefined loaf sugar known in Latin America as *panela, piloncillo, or papelón.* It is available at Hispanic markets. Use a box grater to grate off as much as you need. You can substitute regular brown sugar, but you'll lose something. A good-quality dark muscovado natural cane sugar is a better idea.

This celebrated seventeenth-century formula for drinking chocolate mixed with jasmine was attributed to Francesco Redi, a medical attendant for one of the last Medicis, Cosimo III, Grand Duke of Tuscany. For the original version, dubbed "The Renowned Jasmine Chocolate of the Grand Duke of Tuscany," see the authoritative *The True History of Chocolate* by Sophie and Michael Coe.

# Laurent Tourondel's Cacao Nib Wafers and Rich Custard Ice Cream with Lavender-Vanilla Syrup

*In a new spin on the ideal of tuiles, or thin cookies with ice cream, Laurent Toroundel of Cello pairs a super-creamy frozen custard with crisp, brittle wafers that are almost pure cacao, then offsets the two different intensities with the flowery but slightly resinous accent of a lavender-vanilla syrup and crystallized lavender blossoms.*

• MAKES **6** SERVINGS

## CACAO WAFERS

1/2 cup roasted cacao nibs, preferably a *trinitario*, such as El Rey Carenero Superior or Scharffen Berger

2/3 cup sugar

2 tablespoons glucose syrup, Lyle's Golden Syrup, or light corn syrup

3 tablespoons milk

1/2 cup (1 stick) butter

2 tablespoons cocoa powder, preferably Valrhona

## LAVENDER-VANILLA SYRUP AND CRYSTALLIZED LAVENDER

1 small bunch (2 ounces) fresh (not dried) lavender, both blossoms and leaves

1 1/2 cups sugar

1 cup water

Seeds from 1 plump vanilla bean, split lengthwise and scraped

1 egg white, lightly beaten

## ICE CREAM

1 cup heavy cream

1 cup whole milk

1/2 cup sugar

Seeds from 1 vanilla bean, split lengthwise and scraped

6 egg yolks

To make the wafers, chop the cacao nibs until they are the consistency of coarse bread crumbs with a heavy sharp knife or by pulsing in a food procesor.

Combine the sugar, syrup, milk, and butter in a small saucepan and heat over medium heat, stirring constantly, until the sugar is completely dissolved. The mixture should be hot but not near boiling (about 190°F). Whisk in the cocoa powder until smooth, then stir in the chopped cacao nibs.

Quickly turn out the mixture onto the center of a baking sheet lined with parchment paper.

Place another layer of parchment on top of the mass and, using a rolling pin, roll out the mixture between the parchment layers until it is as thin as possible, forming a rectangle a little more than 9 x 12 inches. If the sides of the pan make it too difficult to use a rolling pin, roll and/or press the waffle dough with a plain glass tumbler. Slide the baking sheet into the freezer and chill for 1 hour.

Preheat the oven to 330°F. Remove the baking sheet from the freezer and peel off the top layer of parchment. Bake the cacao nib mixture for 18 to 20 minutes, until very bubbly.

Let the mixture cool slightly. With a small sharp knife, cut the still-warm rectangle into twelve 3 x 3-inch squares. Carefully peel off the remaining parchment paper. Let the wafers cool to room temperature. They can be made as much as 2 days ahead and stored in an airtight container, but they are best used the same day.

To make the lavender syrup and blossoms, pull some of the lavender blossoms from the sprigs to use for the crystallized garnish, reserving between 4 and 8 per serving. Set aside.

In a small heavy saucepan, dissolve 1 cup plus 2 tablespoons of the sugar in the water. Bring to a boil over high heat, reduce the heat to medium, and cook, uncovered, until reduced by about one-third. Remove from the heat; immediately stir the vanilla seeds and all the remaining lavender into the hot syrup. Let stand until completely cool.

While the syrup cools, place the remaining 6 tablespoons of sugar in a small shallow dish.

Carefully dip the lavender blossoms into the beaten egg white (tweezers are handy for this), let the excess drip off, and roll the blossoms in the sugar. Remove to a small plate and let dry for about 1 hour. Strain the cooled syrup through a fine-mesh sieve into a bowl or pitcher. Reserve the crystallized blossoms and syrup while you make the ice cream.

To make the ice cream, preheat the oven to 320°F. Set aside a 1 1/2-quart to 2-quart baking dish that is at least 2 inches deep. Prepare to make a hot water bath by having ready a kettle of boiling water and a baking pan large enough to hold the baking dish.

Combine the cream, milk, sugar, and vanilla seeds in a heavy medium-sized saucepan. Bring to a boil over medium-high heat, stirring occasionally to dissolve the sugar.

While the cream mixture heats, whisk the egg yolks in a mixing bowl just until smooth. As soon as the cream mixture reaches a boil, remove from the heat and slowly add it to the egg yolks, stirring constantly with a wooden spoon. Pour the mixture back into the saucepan. Reduce the heat to low and cook for 4 to 5 minutes, stirring constantly, until it thickens enough to coat the back of a spoon. At once, before it can curdle, strain the thickened custard through a fine-mesh sieve into the baking dish.

Place the baking dish in the larger pan, slide it onto the oven shelf, and carefully pour enough boiling water into the larger pan to come a little more than halfway up the sides of the dish. Bake for 45 to 50 minutes.

Lift the baking dish out of the water bath and let cool to room temperature. When it is completely cooled, refrigerate for 2 hours.

Remove the chilled custard from the refrigerator, whisk with a wire whisk until smooth, and freeze in an ice cream machine according to the manufacturer's instructions, processing it only for the shortest time suggested. Because of the high butterfat content and lack of antifreezing agents, it will become unpleasantly hard if overchilled. For the same reason, it should be used at once. You can hold it in the freezer for up to 2 hours if absolutely necessary, but you will have to break up the butterfat by beating it with a wooden spoon or running it briefly in the machine.

To assemble the dessert, set out 6 serving plates. Place 1 wafer on each plate and add a scoop of ice cream. Top with another wafer. Drizzle a ring of syrup around the "sandwich" and decorate each plate with a few crystallized lavender blossoms.

*Variation:* For the wafers, replace half the chopped cacao nibs with ¼ cup of blanched, toasted almonds (toasted on a baking sheet in a preheated 325°F oven for 15 to 20 minutes, until golden brown). Chop to the same consistency as the cacao nibs and proceed with the recipe as directed.

THE NEW TASTE OF CHOCOLATE

# Fran Bigelow's Princess Pudding

*I find that pastry chefs who have worked for a long time with one brand of chocolate are usually reluctant to try a new one. Not Fran Bigelow! From the first time she tasted the fruity El Rey Bucare from Venezuela she started looking for ways to incorporate it into her repertoire. In this simple but creamy, intensely chocolatey dessert, Fran lets the intrinsic qualities of Bucare do the talking. Serve it either on its own as a sensational pudding or as the filling in a tart.*

• MAKES **6** TO **8** SERVINGS

1¼ cups heavy cream

¼ cup sugar

½ vanilla bean

5 egg yolks

7 ounces dark chocolate, preferably El Rey Bucare (58.5% cacao), finely chopped

1 prebaked 9-inch tart shell (page 142, or any pâte brisée or pâte sucrée shell will do), optional

In a small saucepan, heat the cream and sugar over medium heat. Split the vanilla bean lengthwise with a small sharp knife and scrape out the seeds into the cream mixture; add the scraped bean, stirring to dissolve the sugar. Remove the mixture from the heat just before it comes to a boil.

In a mixing bowl, beat the egg yolks with a whisk. Slowly add the hot cream mixture, whisking constantly until smooth. Return the mixture to the pan over medium-low heat. Cook, stirring constantly, until it just begins to thicken to a custard (170°F on an instant-read thermometer). Do not overcook or it will curdle. Remove from the heat and add the chocolate, whisking just until melted. Remove the vanilla bean and discard.

While the mixture is still warm and liquid, pour into a serving dish (or tart shell). Let cool to room temperature (always best for bringing out chocolate's flavors). If you are not serving within a few hours, refrigerate the pudding (or tart) for up to 1 to 2 days, but be sure to let it warm to room temperature before serving.

# Creamy Chocolate Cheese Flan with Hibiscus Caramel

*This sophisticated flan combines the flowery, fruity, slightly musky acidity of "Jamaica flowers" (the same dried hibiscus calyces that give Red Zinger tea its color and that are used for cooling drinks everywhere in the Caribbean) with the complementary fruitiness of Scharffen Berger dark chocolate, and uses just a little cream cheese to tame and mellow these two different intense flavors. It is not so different from the cream-cheese/fruit paste pairing that Latins like in other contexts. To me, the glistening reddish brown caramel surface hints at something dark and elusive in the whole.*

*For this recipe, do not use the spice marketed as "cinnamon" in American stores (it's really cassia). Look for the soft, flaky true cinnamon from Ceylon, which has a much subtler and more delicate flavor. You can find it in Hispanic markets under the name* canela.

• MAKES ABOUT **12** SERVINGS

### HIBISCUS CARAMEL

1 ounce (about ³/₄ cup) dried hibiscus blossoms (Jamaica flowers)

2 cups water

1 cup sugar

### FLAN

4¹/₂ cups fresh whole milk

1 (14-ounce) can condensed milk

¹/₄ cup dark aged rum

6 star anise pods

2 (3-inch) sticks true cinnamon (soft Ceylon cinnamon, sold as *canela* in Hispanic markets)

1 teaspoon aniseeds

1 teaspoon pure vanilla extract, preferably Mexican

1 teaspoon bitter almond extract

2 plump Mexican vanilla beans, split lengthwise, seeds scraped and reserved

Pinch of freshly grated nutmeg

¹/₈ teaspoon salt

6 ounces Scharffen Berger dark chocolate (70% cacao), finely chopped

6 ounces cream cheese, warmed to room temperature

6 egg yolks

2 whole eggs

To make the caramel, set aside a 10 x 2-inch round cake pan or twelve 4-ounce ramekins. Place the dried hibiscus blossoms in a small pan with the water and bring to a boil over medium heat. Reduce the heat to low and simmer, stirring occasionally, until the calyces are softened and the water is a brilliant ruby red, about 10 minutes. Strain through a fine-mesh sieve into a second small saucepan, pressing with a spoon to extract as much liquid as possible. You will have about 1¼ cups hibiscus infusion.

Add the sugar to the strained infusion and cook over medium heat, watching carefully for about 12 to 14 minutes, until the mixture thickens to look like a syrup, bubbles quickly, and turns a light mahogany color. Now you must work quickly and judge carefully because the coloring makes it tricky to follow the stages from caramelized to scorched. Place a small bowl of cold water by the stove and begin to test by drizzling a drop of the syrup into it every minute or so. For the first 6 minutes, the drops will form a soft ball when pressed between thumb and forefinger; the sugar is done when the drop forms hard brittle threads. The color will be a deep, rich, reddish mahogany. Quickly pour the hot caramel into the cake pan (or ramekins) and swirl to coat the bottom and sides evenly before the mixture hardens. Set aside the pan or ramekins and let cool while you make the flan.

To make the flan, combine the whole milk and condensed milk in a saucepan. Add the rum, star anise, cinnamon sticks, aniseeds, vanilla and almond extracts, vanilla beans, nutmeg, and salt. Bring barely to boil, reduce the heat to low, and simmer gently for 2 to 3 minutes. Add the chocolate, stirring with a wooden spoon to help it melt and blend. Don't worry if you see little unmelted clumps dotting the surface—this is the result of the Scharffen Berger high cacao butter content and will disappear when the other ingredients are added. Remove from the heat and let the spiced chocolate mixture cool to room temperature. When the mixture is cool, remove the vanilla bean, cinnamon sticks, and star anise with a fork or slotted spoon.

Meanwhile, preheat the oven to 335°F. Set up a hot water bath by having ready a kettle of boiling water and a baking dish large enough to hold the cake pan (or ramekins).

With a wooden spoon, beat the cream cheese in a large mixing bowl until softened. Beat in the yolks and whole eggs one at a time, using a whisk or electric mixer. Slowly add the cooled chocolate mixture, whisking to blend completely. Strain the mixture through a medium-mesh strainer directly into the cake pan or ramekins coated with caramel. Place the pan or ramekins in the larger baking dish, slide into the oven, and carefully pour in enough hot water to come halfway up the outside of the cake pan or ramekins.

Bake for about 1 hour (30 to 40 minutes for the ramekins). Don't expect the custard to be completely set in the center. Remove from the oven, lift from the water bath, and let cool to room temperature. Refrigerate in the pan for at least 3 hours before turning the flan out onto a platter (or individual dishes).

*Variation:* For a creamy, rich chocolate ice cream, proceed with the same recipe. Cool the flan overnight. The following day, scoop the flan and the melted caramel into the container of an ice cream machine and process according to manufacturer's instructions. Freeze for about 1 hour for optimum flavor and a creamy texture. Makes about 4½ quarts ice cream.

# Caramelized Chocolate Bread Pudding
## with Coffee-Rum Sauce

*Bread pudding is usually loved as a placid and undemanding comfort food. But my version has the solid, grownup kind of comfort that wakes you up instead of snuggling you off to nursery dreamland. It is as real as bread, as elegant as Venezuelan chocolate, as bracing as strong coffee, to say nothing of all the subtly blended aromas of rum and spices as well as the unexpected crunch contributed by a good dollop of cashews.*

• MAKES **8** TO **10** SERVINGS

## BREAD PUDDING

2 cups sugar

$^1/_3$ cup water

$^1/_2$ cup aged Venezuelan dark rum or Bacardi Premium Black rum

$3^1/_2$ ounces (about $^1/_2$ cup) dark raisins

$2^1/_2$ cups fresh whole milk

1 (14-ounce) can condensed milk

1 tablespoon aniseeds

4 (3-inch) sticks true cinnamon (soft Ceylon cinnamon, sold as *canela* in Hispanic markets)

6 allspice berries

12 ounces El Rey Bucare dark chocolate (58.5% cacao), finely chopped

6 tablespoons unsalted butter, cut into bits

2 cups freshly brewed Cuban-style espresso coffee (see Note) or other strong black coffee

$^1/_4$ teaspoon salt

5 whole eggs

2 egg yolks

1 tablespoon pure vanilla extract, preferably Mexican

1 teaspoon almond extract

1 medium-sized loaf (about 7 ounces) day-old Cuban, French, or Italian bread, cut into 1- to $1^1/_2$-inch cubes (about 7 cups)

3 ounces (about $^3/_4$ cup) unsalted cashew nuts, coarsely chopped

## COFFEE-RUM SAUCE

1 cup heavy cream

1 (14-ounce) can condensed milk

$1^1/_4$ cups freshly brewed Cuban-style espresso (see Note) or other strong black coffee

$^1/_4$ cup aged dark Venezuelan rum or Bacardi Premium Black rum

To make the caramel, have ready a 9 x 13-inch heatproof glass or ceramic baking dish. Combine the sugar and water in a small saucepan and cook over medium-low heat until the sugar is a golden caramel color. At once pour the hot caramel into the dish and swirl quickly to cover the bottom and sides evenly. Set aside.

Preheat the oven to 350°F.

In a small bowl, pour the rum over the raisins and let stand for 30 minutes.

Meanwhile, heat the whole milk and condensed milk in a small saucepan with the aniseeds, cinnamon, and allspice. Bring to a boil, reduce the heat to low, and simmer for about 10 minutes until the milk is infused with the spices.

Combine the chocolate and butter in a large mixing bowl. Strain the hot milk into the bowl through a fine-mesh strainer and stir to dissolve the chocolate and butter. Stir in the coffee and salt.

In a medium-sized mixing bowl, whisk the whole eggs and egg yolks with the vanilla and almond extracts. Stir into the warm chocolate mixture. Add the cubed bread, rum-soaked raisins, and cashews and toss to distribute evenly. Let stand for 1 hour, until the bread has absorbed the liquid. Mash with a fork or potato masher to break up large pieces of crust.

Pour the bread mixture into the caramel-coated baking dish. Bake for 40 to 45 minutes, or until just set but still slightly loose (the internal temperature should be about 175° to 180°F). Turn out onto a platter. At this point, the

pudding may be tightly covered in plastic wrap and refrigerated for 2 to 3 days, then brought to room temperature before serving.

To make the sauce, bring the cream to a boil in a small saucepan and cook over medium heat, watching carefully, until reduced by half. Stir in the condensed milk, coffee, and rum and heat just until the mixture almost boils. Remove from the heat and let cool to room temperature. The sauce will also keep in the refrigerator for 2 to 3 days.

To serve, cut the pudding while still warm or at room temperature into squares. Serve with the sauce spooned over.

*Note:* For the coffee, you can use a regular drip coffee maker and any good coffee, doubling the amount to obtain a very dark brew that will be close enough to what Cubans call espresso.

# Angela Arzave's
# Omanhene Chocolate–Coconut Custard Stack

*Angela Arzave, the pastry chef of San Francisco's Bacar Restaurant and Wine Salon, loves to experiment with different chocolates. She created this opulent layered custard as a showcase for Omanhene chocolate from Ghana, the only commercial chocolate manufactured on the African continent. Angela serves the dessert accompanied by crisp florentines. This version of the recipe is my adaptation.*

• MAKES **16** SERVINGS

## COCONUT CUSTARD

2$^1$/$_2$ **cups heavy cream**

2 **cups whole milk**

3 **cups (8 ounces) toasted sweetened flaked coconut**

12 **egg yolks**

2 **whole eggs**

$^1$/$_2$ **cup sugar**

3 **ounces (about** $^3$/$_4$ **cup) blanched almonds, very finely ground (about** $^1$/$_2$ **cup after grinding)**

## CHOCOLATE CUSTARD

12 **ounces Omanhene milk chocolate (48% cacao), finely chopped**

2$^1$/$_2$ **cups heavy cream**

1$^1$/$_2$ **cups whole milk**

12 **egg yolks**

## CHOCOLATE TOPPING

3 **ounces Omahene milk chocolate (48% cacao), finely chopped**

Preheat the oven to 300°F. Line a 9 x 12-inch baking dish with a piece of greased heavy-duty foil long enough to overhang the dish at least 3 inches on each end. Set up a hot water bath by having ready a a kettle of boiling water and a baking pan large enough to hold the baking dish.

In a small saucepan, bring the cream and milk to a boil over medium heat. Remove from the heat and add the coconut; cover the pan and let stand for about 15 minutes.

Strain the coconut-infused cream mixture through a fine-mesh strainer, pressing with the back of a spoon to extract as much liquid as possible. Discard the coconut.

In a large mixing bowl, beat the egg yolks and whole eggs with the sugar until pale and creamy. Add a little of the cream mixture and beat to incorporate well before gradually adding the rest, beating to combine.

Pour the mixture into the foil-lined baking dish and sprinkle the ground almonds evenly over the top. Place the baking dish in the larger baking pan and slide into the oven. Carefully pour enough boiling water into the outside pan to come halfway up the outside of the baking dish. Bake for about 80 minutes, or until the custard is fairly set but still jiggles slightly when touched; do not overbake (custard should not be solidly firm).

Lift the pan out of the water bath and set aside to cool. Let it come to room temperature before you make the chocolate custard.

To make the chocolate custard, have ready a large bowl or saucepan of cracked ice floating in a little water. In the top of a double boiler or in a heatproof medium-sized bowl that will fit over a saucepan, warm the chocolate over simmering water until thoroughly melted.

In a small saucepan, bring the cream and milk to a boil over medium heat; remove from the heat.

In a medium-sized mixing bowl, gently stir the egg yolks with a whisk. Add a little of the hot cream mixture, whisking vigorously; then whisk the yolks into the rest of the cream until very smooth. Add the mixture to the chocolate in the top of the double boiler and whisk to combine thoroughly.

Increase the heat under the double boiler to medium. Cook, stirring, until the temperature of the chocolate custard reaches 170°F and hold it at that temperature for 3 to 4 minutes, stirring constantly. Quickly set the double-boiler top in the bowl of cracked ice and stir constantly until the custard is chilled. Pour the chocolate custard over the coconut custard in the baking pan. Refrigerate overnight.

To make the topping, melt the 3 ounces of chocolate in the top of a double boiler over simmering water. Spread a thin layer of the chocolate over the custard. Return the dish to the refrigerator and let the chocolate harden.

To serve, place a serving platter face down over the top of the baking pan. Grasping both the serving platter and the baking dish, swiftly and carefully invert onto the platter. Lift the baking dish off of the custard. Gently peel off the foil. Cut into 16 pieces and serve.

# Maya-Mediterranean Chocolate Rice Pudding

*In a hole-in-the-wall bookstore in Mérida, Yucatán, I once found a curious little cookbook written long ago by a town historian. It was a gold mine of traditional recipes from another era. My favorite was a simple rice pudding with achiote seeds (also called "annatto") and chocolate. "This is history in a pudding," I said to myself as I read the recipe. Someone in colonial times had the brilliant idea of uniting an ancient Maya chocolate drink dyed with the classic coloring of the New World tropics and a homespun Mediterranean sweet.*

*It has been a part of my repertoire for many years, but I'm not sure the town historian would recognize what I have done with his quiet, simple model. The original had no spices, except for cinnamon, while my version is rich with spices to suit my mood. But no matter what I do with this rich, sultry, red-tawny dish, I always pledge my Latin American allegiance with a can of our indispensable condensed milk. And I always follow my own idea of what a good rice pudding should taste and feel like— perfumed and sensuous, with the grains of rice almost melting into the matrix of the scented milk. For this, I start by cooking the rice in achiote-infused water so that it will soften nicely and take up the orange color of the seeds before I add the milk. My final touch is another bit of New World culinary history: the irresistible note of pure vanilla bean. This is a generous recipe, ideal for entertaining a crowd.*

• MAKES **8** TO **12** SERVINGS

1 cup whole achiote (annatto)
   seeds

10 cups water

1 cup short-grain rice, preferably Spanish

1 tablespoon aniseeds

12 allspice berries

4 (3-inch) sticks true cinnamon
   (soft Ceylon cinnamon,
   sold as *canela* in Hispanic
   markets)

1 dried árbol or serrano chile

2 teaspoons salt

4 cups fresh whole milk

2 (14-ounce) cans condensed
   milk

3 ounces El Rey Bucare dark
   chocolate (58.5% cacao),
   Valrhona Pur Caraïbe dark
   chocolate (66% cacao), or
   other fruity dark chocolate,
   finely chopped

2 plump Mexican vanilla beans

Ground true cinnamon (soft Ceylon cinnamon,
   sold as *canela* in Hispanic markets) for
   dusting

ABOVE: Achiote

THE NEW TASTE OF CHOCOLATE

Place the achiote in a medium-sized saucepan and cover with the water. Bring to a gentle boil and simmer, uncovered, for 5 minutes. Strain through a fine-mesh sieve into a bowl and set aside. (You can save the achiote seeds and reuse them for another purpose by again steeping in hot liquid.)

Meanwhile, rinse the rice under cold running water until the water runs clear. Set aside to drain well in a sieve or colander. Tie the aniseeds, allspice, cinnamon sticks, and dried chile in a piece of cheesecloth.

Pour the reserved achiote water into a heavy-bottomed 5- or 6-quart saucepan. Add the drained rice, spice bouquet, and salt. Bring to a boil, reduce the heat to medium, and cook, uncovered, until the rice is soft, 20 to 25 minutes.

Stir in the whole milk and condensed milk. Reduce the heat to low and cook for 5 minutes. Add the chocolate, stirring with a wooden spoon to mix evenly as it melts. Cook, uncovered, for another 40 minutes, stirring occasionally; it should be very creamy but not dry. Halfway through the cooking, split the vanilla beans lengthwise with a small sharp knife and scrape the seeds into the mixture. Add the scraped beans and stir to mix well.

When the pudding is done but still a little loose-textured, remove and discard the spice bouquet and vanilla beans. Pour into a serving dish, dust lightly with the ground cinnamon, and serve warm or at room temperature. Cacao Nib Wafers (see page 150) are a good accompaniment.

# Pierre Hermé's Chocolate Croquettes with Coconut, Pistachio, and Pearl Tapioca Sauce

*The renowned Parisian pâtissier Pierre Hermé is known for both his technical virtuosity and his keen intellect. Though he is a product of the French workhorse discipline that is the hallmark of schooled pastry chefs, he belongs also to another rare breed—the "philosopher chef." He is curious about everything, able to immerse himself in the exigencies of ingredients he loves, and willing to try effects that shake up our preconceptions. Think of him as a modern alchemist distilling magic from noble and mundane ingredients. When I met Pierre to discuss this recipe, he spoke passionately of his devotion to single-origin chocolates, especially those from a small Roanne manufacturer named François Pralus. For him, working with chocolate means exploring examples that are as individual in their compositions as great wines from extremely diverse estates.*

• MAKES **8** SERVINGS

**LIGHTLY CANDIED GINGER**

$1/4$ cup sugar

$1/2$ to $2/3$ cup water ($1/2$ cup plus 2 tablespoons)

Small chunk of fresh ginger (about 2 ounces), peeled and finely julienned

**COCONUT-PISTACHIO-TAPIOCA SAUCE**

$1/3$ cup medium-sized pearl tapioca, not minute or instant

$1 1/2$ ounces pistachio paste (available from professional baking suppliers)

2 ounces flavored tinted pistachio paste

2 cups whole milk

2 tablespoons to $1/2$ cup sugar, or to taste (amount depends on whether sweetened or unsweetened pistachio paste is used)

Zest of $1/4$ orange, in 1 or 2 long strips

3 ($1/8$-inch-thick) slices fresh ginger

$1 3/4$ cups fresh or canned unsweetened coconut milk

$1/2$ cup heavy cream, scalded (increase to 1 cup for a thinner sauce)

**CROQUETTES**

$1/2$ small Scotch bonnet or habanero chile, very finely minced

8 tablespoons (1 stick) melted unsalted butter, kept warm

5 ounces François Pralus Madagascar dark chocolate (75% cacao) or Valrhona Manjari dark chocolate (66% cacao), finely chopped

3 egg yolks

4 whole eggs

2 tablespoons sugar

$2 1/2$ cups freshly grated coconut or unsweetened coconut flakes

Vegetable oil for deep frying (canola oil works fine)

$1/2$ cup canned corn kernels, drained

To candy the ginger, bring the sugar and water to a boil over medium-high heat. Add the ginger, decrease the heat to low, and cook for 20 minutes, until it is translucent and the syrup has thickened. Transfer to a small bowl, cover, and refrigerate.

To make the sauce, place the tapioca pearls in a small bowl. Cover with cold water and let soak for 25 minutes. In a saucepan, thin the pistachio pastes with the milk. Add the tapioca, sugar, orange zest, ginger, and coconut milk. Cook over low heat for 20 minutes, Remove the orange zest and the ginger slices. Add the cream and mix to combine thoroughly. Transfer to a container, cover the surface with plastic wrap, and refrigerate until well chilled, about 2 hours.

To make the croquettes, first prepare the mold. Coat a shallow 5 x 5-inch container (plastic or disposable aluminum will work) with vegetable spray. Line with plastic wrap and set aside. Alternatively, you can make a mold by cutting cardboard into four 5-inch-long, 1-inch-wide strips, and one 5-inch square. Assemble the pieces into a 4-sided mold with a bottom, securing the seams with masking tape. Line with plastic wrap, spray with oil, and set aside.

Sauté the chile in 1 tablespoon of the butter over high heat for about 1 minute. In the top of a double boiler, combine the remaining butter, the chocolate, and the chile. Cover and melt almost completely over hot, not boiling water. Stir until smooth.

In a medium bowl, whisk the egg yolks, 1 whole egg, and the sugar until the sugar has dissolved. Add the melted chocolate and whisk until smooth. Pour the mixture into the mold and freeze until solidly frozen, 2 to 3 hours. Line a baking sheet with parchment paper. Place the remaining 3 whole eggs in a small bowl and beat lightly. Place $1^1/_2$ cups of the coconut in a separate bowl.

Invert the frozen mixture onto a cutting board, and remove the mold and plastic wrap. Cut into 25 1-inch squares, wiping the blade after each cut. Evenly coat 1 square in the beaten egg, then roll in the grated coconut and set on the baking sheet. Repeat with the other squares. Freeze for 30 minutes, until firm. Place the remaining coconut in a clean bowl. Coat the squares again with egg and coconut. No chocolate should be visible through the coating. Freeze again for at least 30 minutes.

Heat 4 inches of oil to 338°F in a heavy-bottomed pot. Using a slotted spoon, lower 5 squares into the oil. Fry until light golden, about $1^1/_2$ minutes. Drain on paper towels. Repeat with the remaining squares.

To serve, place $^1/_2$ cup of the sauce in 8 shallow bowls. Scatter 1 tablespoon of corn over the sauce. Arrange 3 croquettes over the sauce. Garnish with the candied ginger, and serve.

*Variation:* The sauce can also be made with whole pistachios. Substitute $^1/_2$ cup shelled unsalted pistachios for the pastes. Finely chop the nuts and $^1/_2$ cup sugar in a food processor. Bring nuts, sugar, and milk to a boil, then turn off heat and steep for 25 minutes. Strain into a saucepan, add the drained tapioca, orange zest, ginger, and coconut milk. Bring to a gentle boil, then simmer for about 20 minutes. Finish sauce as directed in recipe.

# Mary Cech's Onyx Chocolate–Coconut Soup with Fresh Bananas and Honey-Cocoa Wafers

*This inventive dessert soup comes from the experienced pastry chef Mary Cech, who teaches at the Napa Valley branch of the Culinary Institute of America. Like many chefs now experimenting with chocolate, she plays up its affinity for other tropical treats, such as coconuts and banana.*

*Hot soups, like hot chocolate, allow the full bouquet of the chocolate to emerge. Mary's choice, the dark bittersweet Onyx from San Francisco manufacturer Guittard, is a blend using Ivory Coast cacao for clean chocolate flavor and Ecuadorian cacao for flowery notes, with an intense fruity, lingering finish contributed by Carenero Superior beans from Venezuela. Nonalkalized cocoa powder will produce tan-colored wafers, and Dutch-process cocoa makes richer, darker ones.*

• MAKES **4** SERVINGS

## HONEY-COCOA WAFERS

1 cup all-purpose flour

2 tablespoons cocoa powder

9 tablespoons (1 stick plus 1 tablespoon) unsalted butter, softened to room temperature

1/2 cup granulated sugar

1/4 cup confectioners' sugar plus more, for dusting

1/2 cup honey

5 large or 6 medium egg whites

## SOUP

4 ounces Guittard Onyx dark chocolate (70% cacao), finely chopped

1 cup canned unsweetened coconut milk

2 tablespoons coconut syrup, preferably Monin brand

2/3 cup sweet dessert wine, such as Beaumes-de-Venise, vin santo, or sweet sherry

4 tablespoons (1/2 stick) salted butter

2 tablespoons sugar

1 banana, sliced

To make the wafers, preheat the oven to 325°F. Have ready two 17 x 12-inch sheet pans. Cut into 17 x 12-inch parchment paper rectangles, butter lightly, and set aside.

Sift the flour and cocoa powder together and set aside. In the bowl of an electric mixer fitted with the paddle attachment, cream the butter, granulated sugar, confectioners' sugar, and honey at medium speed until smooth, scraping down the bowl as needed. Decrease the speed to low and gradually add the egg whites, incorporating each well before adding the next. Mix until the egg whites are completely blended in. The mixture will look slightly curdled. Add the sifted flour and cocoa mixture. Mix on low speed, scraping the bowl as needed, until the mixture is smooth and homogeneous, about 45 seconds.

Place one parchment sheet flat on the work surface. Using a small offset spatula, spread 1 cup of batter thinly and evenly into a large 11 x 16-inch rectangle. Pick up the ends of the batter-coated parchment and transfer it to a baking sheet. Bake for 7 to 9 minutes or until the wafer batter is firm to the touch, shiny, and slightly brown at the edges. Remove from the oven and slide the parchment from the baking sheet onto the work surface. Run a spatula under the edge of the wafer and loosen it, but do not remove from the parchment. Cool on a flat surface. Let the baking sheet cool before proceeding.

Repeat the process 4 times, each time spreading the batter onto a fresh parchment sheet, until you have 5 rectangles of wafers. When cool enough to handle, break the wafers into irregular pieces and dust lightly with confectioners' sugar. The batter may be prepared up to 3 days ahead, and the wafers may be baked up to 6 hours before serving.

To make the soup, combine the chocolate and coconut milk in the top of a double boiler over simmering water and stir until the chocolate is melted. Add the coconut syrup, wine, butter, and sugar. Stir until the butter and sugar are smoothly dissolved.

To serve, ladle into soup bowls, allowing 1$^1$/$_2$ cups per serving. Add a few slices of

banana to each bowl. Serve with the Honey-Cocoa Wafers.

*Variations:* For a variation on the wafers, try curling them or, as one tester did, try baking them in a smaller pan to create a spongy brownie. For curls, follow the instructions as given, but after 3 minutes of baking, remove from the oven and cut the wafers into 3-inch-wide ribbons with a pizza cutter. Return the pan to the oven and continue baking until firm. To shape, quickly lift each ribbon from the parchment and roll it around a jar or rolling pin while still hot. When ribbons are cool, dust lightly with confectioners' sugar. To make brownies, spread the batter in a 9 x 13-inch pan and bake for 10 minutes or until no longer sticky when pressed with a fingertip. Cool for at least 20 minutes before cutting.

## TRADITIONAL HANDMADE CHOCOLATE

Throughout Latin America, cacao is the basis of a small cottage industry controlled by women—the making of rustic cacao balls and bars for hot chocolate. The technique of grinding the roasted cacao beans on a *metate,* perfected in Mesoamerica by the Maya and Aztecs, traveled everywhere that cacao was turned into chocolate for drinking, starting sometime in the sixteenth century. Today, not everyone in Latin America subscribes to the back-breaking *metate.* In Chuao, an isolated town in Venezuela's central Aragua coast, the children in the family help their mother grind the roasted cacao nibs in a sturdy corn grinder. When I suggested to one of the women that she add some spices to her cacao bars and balls as the women of the Paria Peninsula do, she said that flavorings would spoil the taste of Chuao's cacao, which, she added, "is the best in the world."

LEFT: Ana Rodríguez grinds cacao nibs and half a dozen spices in a motorized corn grinder in Yaguaraparo, Venezuela.
CENTER: The women of Chuao mix freshly roasted cacao nibs with sugar to manufacture cacao balls and chocolate bars.
RIGHT: Women sell rustic homemade chocolate bars at a market in Pointe-à-Pitre, the capital of the French Caribbean island of Guadeloupe.

THE NEW TASTE OF CHOCOLATE

# Ana Rodríguez's Homemade Cacao Balls in the Style of the Paria Peninsula

*The best artisanal chocolate I know is made by Ana Rodríguez in the dusty northern Venezuelan town of Yaguaraparo in the Paria Peninsula, a hilly finger of land running nearly to the coast of Trinidad. Ana grinds her mixture in enormous quantities, using a motorized grinder perched on the stand of an old sewing machine, and rolls it into grainy-textured balls.*

*Ana's chocolate unites the best of the primitive and the sophisticated, starting with the strong-flavored Río Caribe cacao beans that she dries herself on the street in front of her house. Because the cacao is unfermented, she compensates by roasting the beans very deeply. She uses an adventurous range of spices—some I cannot duplicate, like the vanilla-scented tonka bean and the almondlike mamey sapote (Pouteria sapote). No one flavor dominates; all mingle in delicate equilibrium.*

*To make something like Ana's cacao balls, you need a food processor or heavy mortar and pestle, preferably marble, and a hand-cranked rotary grinder for refining the texture of the cacao nibs. The only type of grinder I have found satisfactory is a Corona aluminumized cast-iron plate mill from Colombia, ordinarily used for grinding corn and available in many Latin American neighborhood stores (see Sources). I also recommend a mini-chopper, a spice or coffee mill, and a scale accurate enough to register fractions of ounces or gradations of a few grams.*

• MAKES **23** OR **24** (1.2-OUNCE) BALLS

1$^1$/$_2$ pounds whole cacao beans (makes about 1 pound roasted and shelled nibs) or 1 pound (about 4 cups) roasted, shelled cacao nibs

1 pound (2$^1$/$_4$ cups) sugar, or to taste

1 quarter-sized slice fresh ginger ($^1$/$_2$ ounce), peeled and minced

$^1$/$_2$ teaspoon almond extract

2 plump vanilla beans

1 teaspoon aniseeds

1 teaspoon allspice berries

6 whole cloves

1 (3-inch) stick true cinnamon (soft Ceylon cinnamon, sold as *canela* in Hispanic markets), coarsely chopped with a knife, or 2 tablespoons ground true cinnamon

$^1$/$_8$ teaspoon freshly grated nutmeg

If you are using whole cacao beans, heat a large (12-inch) griddle, *comal,* or heavy-bottomed skillet over medium heat. Add the cacao beans and roast, stirring constantly, until they develop a deep roasted flavor and a rich brown color. The roasting time will vary according to the size and quality of the beans. Large *criollo* beans of an even size will take about 30 minutes, *forastero* or *trinitario* beans of uneven sizes 35 to 40 minutes. For even-sized *trinitarios,* allow 20 to 25 minutes. In any case, it is advisable to test the beans every 5 minutes or so by breaking one open and tasting it to determine the degree of roasting. It's all a matter of taste.

Place the roasted beans in a tray or bowl and allow to cool. When they are cool enough to handle, shell them one at a time, trying to keep the nibs as whole as possible to avoid waste. From 1 1/2 pounds of *trinitario* cacao of uneven size, you can expect to end up with 18 ounces or less of cacao nibs.

If you are using commercial cacao nibs, taste one to see if they have been roasted enough. If you feel your nibs are underroasted, place them on a heated *comal,* griddle, or heavy-bottomed skillet, and roast over medium heat while stirring for about 5 minutes, or until they are roasted to your liking.

Place the roasted nibs, sugar, ginger, and almond extract in a food processor and process for about 10 minutes, stopping every 2 minutes and letting the machine rest for a few seconds to prevent overheating the motor. The idea is to grind the nibs finely into a thick, warm paste.

Meanwhile, grind the spices. First grind the vanilla beans to a sticky powder in a mini-chopper. Set aside. Next grind the aniseeds, allspice and cloves to a fine powder in a spice mill or coffee mill. Then follow with the cinnamon. Add the vanilla, nutmeg, and the other ground spices to the cacao-sugar mixture and continue processing for 2 to 3 minutes, until all the ingredients are well integrated into a sticky paste.

At this point the cacao mass needs further refining. It must be put through a grinder like a plate corn mill. Add the warm cacao paste in batches through the machine's feed tube while pushing it down with a pestle. Cranking takes some elbow grease, and the machine must be very firmly clamped to a countertop or table. Put the paste through the machine once more to refine further. The cacao mass will still feel coarse (but that's fine for hot chocolate). You'll lose some cacao mass and end up with about 1 pound 11 ounces of the mixture.

To shape the cacao balls, divide the sticky paste into 23 or 24 equal portions of about 1.2 ounces each. If you have warm hands like me, it might help to chill your palms periodically by rubbing them with ice cubes and drying them well. Roll each portion between the palms of your hands to form a ball or a slightly rhomboid shape. (Don't worry if they do not look perfect.) Place the balls on a tray or baking sheet lined with parchment paper. Allow to dry for a couple of hours or more before storing in an airtight container, either in a cool place or in the refrigerator.

## WORLD'S BEST HOT CHOCOLATE

To make Ana Rodríguez's hot chocolate, all you need to do is dissolve 1 cacao ball in 2/3 cup hot milk or water. To obtain a rich head of foam, blend the two with a Mexican *molinillo* (wooden chocolate "mill") or, better still, a hand-held electric immersion blender.

Josefa Ramírez makes classic Mexican chocolate at the celebrated Churrería del Recuerdo in Xalapa, Mexico. After adding hot milk to the cinnamon-spiced chocolate, she twirls a wooden *molinillo* between her palms to whip the mixture to a rich froth.

THE NEW TASTE OF CHOCOLATE

# Aromatic Spice and Corn Blend for Hot Chocolate (Pinole o Polvos de Soconosco)

Pinole *is the name both for a form of ground toasted corn and for a flavorful mixture that also includes spices like vanilla, achiote, and cinnamon ground to a fine powder. It became a well-known flavoring ingredient in Spain and many parts of the colonies. Toasted barley flour, or* máchica, *plays a similar role in Ecuador. Both go into aromatic chocolate porridgelike drinks that would have been familiar to the sixteenth-century observer Juan de Cárdenas, who diligently reported the obsession of budding colonial society with chocolate and the countless new chocolate recipes that seemed to spring from the woodwork. The* pinole *mix makes about 1¼ cups, so you'll have extra to keep on hand.*

• MAKES 1 SERVING

## SPICED PINOLE MIX

2 plump vanilla beans, preferably Mexican, cut into ¼-inch lengths

1 cup *pinole* (toasted ground corn)

1 tablespoon achiote (annatto) seeds

1 tablespoon (about 3 dozen) small allspice berries

2 (3-inch) sticks true cinnamon (soft Ceylon cinnamon, sold as *canela* in Hispanic markets), coarsely chopped with a knife

1 teaspoon aniseeds

## HOT CHOCOLATE

1 cup whole milk

1 ounce Chocovic Guaranda dark chocolate (71% cacao), finely chopped

Pinch of salt

1 tablespoon sugar (optional)

To make the mix, grind the vanilla to a sticky powder in a mini-chopper or spice mill. Combine with the *pinole* in a small bowl; set aside.

Grind the achiote in a spice mill. When it is fairly fine, add the allspice, cinnamon, and aniseeds. Grind to a powder. Combine well with the *pinole*-vanilla mixture. Store at room temperature in a tightly sealed jar.

To make the hot chocolate, bring the milk to a simmer in a small saucepan over medium heat. Add the chocolate and stir with a wooden spoon until it dissolves, about 1 minute. Stir in 1 tablespoon of the spice mix and the salt, then taste and, if desired, sweeten with a little sugar. Keep stirring until the mixture thickens to the consistency of a light porridge or chocolate sauce, 2 to 3 minutes. Serve at once.

# Jim Graham's Spiced Hot Chocolate

*Chicago master chocolatier Jim Graham points out that "hot chocolate is an excellent vehicle for tasting complex chocolates" because as the heat releases volatile aromatic components "every nuance of flavor and aroma is instantly available to the senses." Here he uses dark Valrhona Pur Caraïbe chocolate, commenting, "While Pur Caraïbe can be used by itself for hot chocolate, I find the result a bit austere. Hot chocolate should soothe and comfort the drinker, engage the palate on friendly terms." To do this without adding extra sugar, he uses flavorings like orange zest and ginger for a "psychological" sweetening of the recipe. The salt, although small in dose, is very important to the overall balance.*

• MAKES **1** SERVING

$^1/_4$ **cup heavy cream**

$^1/_2$ **cup milk**

**1 scant teaspoon aniseeds, coarsely crushed in a mortar**

**1 teaspoon finely grated orange zest**

**1 (2-inch) length vanilla bean, split lengthwise, seeds scraped out**

**1 quarter-sized slice fresh ginger**

**1 ounce Valrhona Pur Caraïbe dark chocolate (66% cacao), finely chopped**

**Very small pinch of salt**

In a heavy saucepan set over medium heat, combine the cream, milk, aniseeds, orange zest, vanilla beans and seeds, and ginger. Bring just to a boil. Cover, reduce the heat to very low, and keep at a bare simmer for 10 minutes.

Place the chocolate in a small bowl. Using a fine-mesh strainer, strain a few spoonfuls of the hot cream mixture over the chocolate and whisk with a small wire whisk until the chocolate is completely melted. Strain the rest of the cream mixture over the chocolate, add the salt, and whisk to combine thoroughly before pouring into a serving cup.

THE NEW TASTE OF CHOCOLATE

# "Age of Discovery" Vanilla-Scented Hot Chocolate

The first European treatise on chocolate, written about 125 years after the Spaniards had encountered the fabulous pairing of vanilla and chocolate in Mexico, is Antonio Colmenero de Ledesma's Curioso tratado de la naturaleza y calidad del chocolate (1644).

By the seventeenth century, Spaniards in both Mexico and Spain had put their own stamp on the heady Aztec and Maya beverages. For the sake of Spanish cooks the author suggests substitutes for three of the New World ingredients most commonly used along with vanilla in both pre-Columbian and colonial Mexican recipes for chocolate: a certain type of chile, an edible flower called ueinacaxtli (Chiranthodendron pentadactylon), known also as "ear flowers," and mecasuchil (Piper aurantium, today called hoja santa or acuyo and still indispensable in Veracruzan cooking).

In the original recipe, the whole mass of cacao beans was ground to a paste on a grinding stone (metate) with whole vanilla beans, nuts, and other seasonings, then shaped into balls or cakes to be dissolved in hot water (sometimes milk or almond milk). Here is my version of this famous classic using plump Mexican vanilla beans and modern commercial chocolate made with Venezuelan cacao beans—the ones most likely to have been used in an upscale chocolate drink such as this in seventeenth-century Spain.

• MAKES **8** SERVINGS

8 cups milk or water

¹/₄ cup achiote (annatto) seeds

12 blanched almonds

12 toasted and skinned hazelnuts

2 to 3 vanilla beans (preferably Mexican from Papantla), split lengthwise, seeds scraped out

¹/₄ ounce dried rosebuds (sold as *rosa de Castilla* in Hispanic markets)

2 (3-inch) sticks true cinnamon (soft Ceylon cinnamon, sold as *canela* in Hispanic markets)

1 tablespoon aniseeds

2 whole dried árbol or serrano chiles

8 ounces dark chocolate, preferably El Rey Gran Samán (70% cacao) or Chocovic Ocumare (71% cacao), finely chopped

Pinch of salt

Sugar

1 tablespoon orange-blossom water (optional)

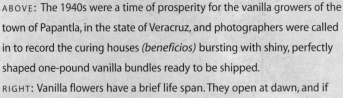

ABOVE: The 1940s were a time of prosperity for the vanilla growers of the town of Papantla, in the state of Veracruz, and photographers were called in to record the curing houses *(beneficios)* bursting with shiny, perfectly shaped one-pound vanilla bundles ready to be shipped.

RIGHT: Vanilla flowers have a brief life span. They open at dawn, and if they are not pollinated by noon, they wither. Using his fingernail, this Totonac worker from Papantla, circa 1930, hand pollinates this hard-to-reach vanilla blossom by bending the rostellum upwards and then transferring the pollen from the anther to the stigma.

In a heavy, medium-sized saucepan, heat the milk with the achiote seeds over medium heat. Bring to a low boil, stirring frequently. Reduce the heat to low and let steep for 10 minutes, until the liquid is brightly dyed with the achiote.

Meanwhile, grind the almonds and hazelnuts to the consistency of fine breadcrumbs, using a mini-chopper or Mouli grater. Set aside.

Strain out the achiote and return the milk to the saucepan. Add the ground nuts along with the vanilla beans and scraped seeds, rosebuds, cinnamon, aniseeds, and chiles. Bring to a low boil. Reduce the heat to low and simmer for about 10 minutes. Remove from the heat; stir in the chocolate and salt. Taste for sweetness and add a little sugar if desired, together with the orange-blossom water. Strain through a fine-mesh strainer.

Transfer the chocolate to a tall narrow pot and whisk vigorously with a Mexican *molinillo* (wooden chocolate mill) or a handheld electric immersion blender. It makes a spectacular frothy head. Serve immediately.

# Kekchi Cacao-Chile Balls

In Alta Verapaz, a lush and deeply forested region of Guatemala that was part of the ancient Mesoamerican chocolate empire, the Kekchi Maya roast cacao beans and grind them with ululte, *the local name for the tiny but devilish* chile piquín. *They shape the resulting sticky paste into balls, which are then air-dried and stored. To add heat and flavor to feast dishes like the* chompipe *(turkey) and* pepianes *(stews thickened with pumpkin seeds), they grate a little of this mixture over the food.*

*I've taken up this exciting idea at home, but I tend to expand on the seasonings. This particular version was inspired by a batch of Papua New Guinea beans that had been dried over wood fires during the rainy season. They were too smoky and hammy for a fine chocolate, but perfect for my purpose. I played up the smokiness with a dash of Spanish smoked paprika and added a little allspice and soft true cinnamon from Mexico.*

*Experiment with other combinations of spices if you wish, or vary the proportions to taste. Once you discover how this magic seasoning wakes up food, you might enjoy passing the cacao balls around the tables with a small cheese grater and letting each person grate his or her own onto the plate. I've used it with lobster stew, slightly sweet cream soups, and different meat stews (lamb, beef, even venison).*

*A powerful mini–food processor is almost essential for grinding the cacao and chile, unless you have a good big marble mortar and pestle or a Mexican* metate.

• MAKES **12** BALLS

3 ounces (about ²/₃ cup) cacao nibs

3 ounces (about 1 cup) piquín chiles

1 (1-inch) stick true cinnamon (soft Ceylon cinnamon, sold as *canela* in Hispanic markets), coarsely chopped

¹/₂ teaspoon allspice berries

1 teaspoon salt

1 teaspoon Spanish smoked paprika

Heat a griddle, medium-sized cast-iron skillet, or Mexican *comal* over medium heat. Add the cacao nibs and dry-roast for 2 minutes, until fragrant, turning constantly with a wooden spoon or spatula. Turn out into another container and set aside.

Add the chiles, cinnamon stick, and allspice berries to the griddle and roast the same way, stirring, for 2 minutes. Scrape into an electric spice mill or coffee grinder with the salt and paprika; grind to a fine powder.

Combine the spice mixture and roasted cacao in a mini–food processor and process into a warm, sticky paste, 3 to 4 minutes, stopping to scrape down the sides of the bowl. Scrape out onto a work surface and shape into 12 small balls. Let sit until thoroughly dried. Store in a tightly sealed jar. When ready to use, grate over any dish of your choice.

The sixteenth-century *Códice Azoyú* is a pictorial chronicle of the political history and chronology of the small kingdom of Tlachinollan, in today's Guerrero state in Mexico. Folio 21 depicts a stylized cacao field in the tributary town of Totomixtlahuacan.

THE NEW TASTE OF CHOCOLATE

# Estela Pérez's Mole Xalapeño

*Moles are a large and very ancient tribe whose name derives from the overall word for sauce* (molli) *in Nahuatl, the language of the Aztecs. There is no single ingredient, except perhaps for chiles, that is common to each and every mole. Chocolate never got near a mole recipe until the seventeenth or eighteenth century, when a convent near Puebla City became known for the eponymous dish* mole poblano *that most people (outside of Mexico) identify today with mole.*

*There are many moles made with chocolate (though more are made without it). The following recipe is my interpretation of one I had in Xalapa, the capital of Veracruz state. Here the gentle, patient Estela Pérez, head cook at Raquel Torres's beloved Churrería del Recuerdo, made me the mole her mother taught her to make in a small town near the capital. The mole resembles the famous one made in nearby Xico, southeast of Xalapa, but it has no tomato and is less spicy. Like all* moles, *it is essentially a sauce that can be a vehicle for different foods. The chocolate creates certain aromatic nuances with a dash of bitterness, while adding a little extra body.*

*Mexicans use moles by adding any meat—precooked or partly cooked—to a large amount of the sauce thinned with broth, and cooking it for a while to marry the flavors. The possible choices include pork, beef, turkey, duck, or chicken, either shredded or cut into bite-sized pieces. Estela also uses her mole to make* enmoladas, *or tortillas dipped in the sauce, rolled around a chicken or pork filling, and topped with more mole, chopped onions, and grated cheese (the dry* queso añejo). *In this country, there is no reason we shouldn't serve mole as an accompanying sauce with any roasted or grilled meat.*

• MAKES ABOUT **6** CUPS UNDILUTED MOLE PASTE

Estela cooking her mole

9 ancho chiles (4 ounces), stemmed and seeded

11 pasilla chiles (4 ounces), stemmed and seeded

12 mulato chiles (4 ounces), stemmed and seeded

1 large white onion, unpeeled

1 medium head of garlic, unpeeled

1 (1-inch) stick true cinnamon (soft Ceylon cinnamon, sold as *canela* in Hispanic markets)

1 teaspoon black peppercorns

1 tablespoon aniseeds

1 medium-sized corn tortilla

1/2 cup (about 2 ounces) dry-roasted peanuts

1/2 cup (about 2 ounces) blanched sliced almonds

1/2 cup (about 2 ounces) hulled green pumpkin seeds

1/2 cup (about 2 ounces) sesame seeds

2/3 cup freshly rendered lard or corn oil

1 medium-sized ripe plantain, peeled and cut into thick slices

1/3 cup (about 2 ounces) pitted prunes

1/2 cup (about 2 ounces) dark raisins

1/3 cup (about 2 ounces) grated *piloncillo* (Latin American brown loaf sugar), dark muscovado natural cane sugar, or old-fashioned-dark brown sugar

3 ounces dark chocolate, preferably El Rey Bucare chocolate (58.5% cacao), any artisanal Mexican chocolate, or Ibarra

1 teaspoon salt

Well-flavored chicken stock

To roast the chiles, wipe them clean with a damp cloth. Heat a large griddle, *comal,* or heavy-bottomed skillet over medium heat. Dry-roast the chiles on the griddle in about 6 batches, allowing about 1 minute on each side and pressing them down with a spatula. Transfer them to a large bowl as they are done; cover with about 1 quart warm water and leave them to soak for about 20 minutes. Drain and reserve 1 cup of the soaking liquid.

Dry-roast the onion and whole head of garlic on the griddle, stirring occasionally, until blackened and blistered, about 8 minutes. Set aside until cool enough to handle.

Lightly dry-roast the cinnamon, black peppercorns, and aniseeds (do not scorch). Grind them to a fine powder in a spice mill or coffee mill and set aside.

Lightly toast the tortilla on the griddle, allowing about 30 seconds per side; set aside. Dry-roast the peanuts, almonds, and pumpkin seeds, stirring or shaking the griddle, for about 1 minute. Set aside in a small bowl. Toast the sesame seeds for about 30 seconds, stirring or shaking the griddle; scrape out into the same bowl. When cool, finely grind the nuts and seeds in a food processor.

Heat the lard or corn oil in a large 12-inch skillet and sauté the plantain slices over medium heat until golden brown. Scoop out with a slotted spoon and let drain on paper towels; set aside the skillet with the fat.

Peel the cooled onion and garlic, chop the onion coarsely, and set aside. Combine all of the roasted ingredients, plantain slices, prunes, and raisins in a large bowl or pot with the reserved chile soaking liquid to thin the mixture just enough for processing into a paste. Process a third of the mixture in a blender or food processor to make a purée. Repeat until all has been processed, adding more soaking liquid as needed.

Heat the reserved lard in the skillet over medium heat. When it ripples, add the purée and cook, stirring, for about 3 minutes, being careful to dodge splatters. Stir in the brown sugar, chocolate, and salt, and cook, stirring, for about 5 minutes.

If you are planning to use this paste at once, dilute it by stirring in good chicken stock until it is as heavy as thin tomato sauce. It isn't absolutely necessary, but the consistency will be much silkier if you force the thinned mixture through a fine-mesh sieve by pushing with a wooden spoon. If you are not using it immediately, cool the mole paste to room temperature, transfer to storage containers, and pour a thin film of melted lard over the surface to help keep it from spoiling. Seal tightly and store it in a cool place or the refrigerator. It will keep well for several months.

Estela assembles the ingredients for her Mole Xalapeño.

# Glossary

**Alkalization:** Treatment of cacao beans (or of chocolate at different stages of the manufacturing process) with an alkali such as potassium carbonate in order to remove unwanted harshness or acidity. This practice allows manufacturers to mask some of the inferior qualities of cheap cacao. By law, the addition of alkali must be indicated on the label. *See also* Dutch-process cocoa.

*Baba:* Spanish for "slime." It refers to the mucilaginous fruit pulp that clings to cacao beans when they are scooped out of the pod. At this stage, the fresh beans are generally referred to as "cacao en baba."

**Bean count:** Estimation of bean size, using the weight of one hundred beans as an average.

**Bittersweet or semisweet chocolate:** Sweetened chocolate containing at least 35 percent cacao liquor (i.e., ground cacao mass) by weight.

**Bloom:** The gray-white film that sometimes appears on the surface of chocolate. It can reflect imperfect tempering of the chocolate or originate when the chocolate undergoes changes in temperature (cacao butter bloom) or is exposed to excess humidity (sugar bloom, caused by crystallization of sugar).

**Bulk beans:** Cacao beans of average to poor quality, used to add cacao mass to manufactured chocolate. More than 90 percent of the world's cacao supply is bulk beans. All bulk cacao is of the *forastero* type. *See also* Flavor beans.

**Cacao beans:** The seeds of the cacao pod. In Spanish there is a distinction between *semillas* (the fresh seeds capable of reproducing) and *almendras* (the seeds after the drying process, ready to be made into chocolate).

**Cacao (cocoa) butter:** The waxy ivory-yellow fat obtained from dried and roasted cacao beans; solid at room temperature. It exhibits not one but several different crystal forms on solidifying after being melted and is the major reason for the great technical difficulties chocolate presents to cooks and confectioners. *See also* Tempering.

**Cacao pods:** The large colorful seed vessels of the cacao tree *(Theobroma cacao)*. The thickness and hardness of the husk varies according to type, with *criollo* cacao having the most fragile exterior, *forastero* the thickest and toughest.

*Cherelle:* French for "immature cacao pod."

*Chirel:* Spanish for "immature cacao pod."

**Chocolate liquor:** In chocolate processing, the ground mass of cacao beans. Also called "cacao liquor" or "cocoa liquor."

*Chupón:* Spanish for "shoot" or "sucker," a secondary branch that must be pruned from the trunk of a cacao tree to concentrate fruit production in the main trunk.

**Clone:** Offspring of a plant produced asexually by grafting slips or buds of the desired parent onto a prepared rootstock. All clones are exact genetic copies of the parent plant.

**Cocoa powder:** The product made by pressing nearly all the cacao butter from chocolate liquor. The remaining solids form a compacted cake ("press cake"), which is then ground to a powder. When untreated with alkali, cocoa powder is light in color and retains much of the flavor of the original beans.

**Compound coating:** Chocolate substitute or analog used in confectionery to bypass the expense and technical difficulty of using real chocolate as a coating. Some varieties contain at least some cacao liquor combined with hydrogenated soybean and/or cottonseed oil; others have cocoa powder combined with highly saturated fats (valued in this case for their high melting points), such as palm oil or coconut oil.

**Conching:** A crucial step in the chocolate manufacturing process that consists of agitating the refined, sweetened chocolate mass at a temperature of 120° to 200°F in a mixer-kneader known as a conche. Conching can last from four hours (with cheaper brands) to seventy-two hours, though recent improvements in conche construction have somewhat shortened the time. The process has several complex physical and chemical effects that operate to mellow the flavor and smooth the texture of chocolate. Any extra cacao butter and all or a percentage of the lecithin used as an emulsifier are usually added during conching. The best conches are open on top to allow maximum aeration of the mass and proper evaporation of harsh, acidic volatile components.

**Couverture:** French for "covering" or "coating." In English, this word is used in a nontechnical sense to indicate any high-quality chocolate for cooking or eating. Originally it referred to fine chocolate primarily used for coating truffles or candies. In France, the minimum cacao content allowed by law for dark chocolate couvertures is 32 percent.

**Cut test:** Standard method of evaluating the quality of cacao-bean shipments by cutting a sampling of beans (one hundred to three hundred) open lengthwise and noting evidence of underfermentation (purple beans), no fermentation (flat, slaty beans), insect damage, mold, or other flaws.

***Criollo* cacao:** A race of cacao that originated in northern South America and is considered the standard of fine chocolate flavor. The interior of the bean is pure white to very light pink. *Criollo* commands the highest prices on the international market.

**Deodorization:** Vacuum process used to remove the characteristic odors of chocolate from cacao butter by the use of steam, making the fat suitable for more purposes and helping manufacturers to produce a uniform product with cacao butter from various origins and mixed-quality beans. It enables manufacturers to use poor-quality, alkali-treated beans, which would produce virtually unpalatable cacao butter if not deodorized. Butter from quality beans retains some of the pleasant flavor and aroma of the cacao solids without deodorization.

**Dipping:** Process of coating truffles or other candies by submerging them in melted chocolate or a substitute; also called "enrobing." Because of chocolate's unique melting properties, hand-dipping is one of the most technically demanding steps in confectionery.

**Dutch-process cocoa:** Cocoa treated with an alkali such as potassium carbonate to neutralize some of the harsh acid components of the original cacao. The color of the alkalized cocoa is quite dark, but the flavor is much milder than that of cocoa made by other methods.

**Estate chocolate:** Chocolate made with cacao beans grown on a single plantation. The term does not necessarily mean that the product is made from only one variety of cacao.

**Exclusive-derivation chocolate:** A broad category that encompasses a wide range of terms used by manufacturers to emphasize the variety or unique provenance of the cacao beans used in their products. *See also* Single-origin and single-variety chocolate.

## Sources

### CHOCOLATE COMPANIES

**Barry Callebaut USA Inc.**
1500 Suckle Highway
Pennsauken, NJ 08110
(800) 774-9131 • (856) 663-2260 • (856) 665-0474 (fax)
www.barry-callebaut.com

This chocolate giant created from a Swiss-engineered merger between the French Cacao Barry and the Belgian Callebaut in 1996 produces a wide range of chocolate couvertures of consistent quality. In 1999, the company introduced Cacao Barry's single-origin couvertures made with bulk beans from the Dominican Republic, Ecuador, and Indonesia, and *trinitarios* from Papua New Guinea. This was followed by the line "Origine rare," with a single introductory product: a 70% couverture made exclusively with beans from the humid Baracoa region in northeastern Cuba.

**Chocolates El Rey C.A.**
*Caracas Corporate Office:*
011 58 212 242 44 51 • 011 58 212 241 12 50 (fax)
*U.S. Representative:*
**El Rey America, Inc.**
P.O. Box 853
Fredericksburg, TX 78624
(800) EL-REY-99 • (830) 997-2200 • (830) 997-2417 (fax)
www.chocolate-elrey.com

Established in 1929, this respected Venezuelan company put the concept of single-origin couvertures on the chocolate map in 1995, under the leadership of Venezuelan-born Jorge Redmond Schlageter. The first modern chocolate plant in a Latin American country, it marries the best of the colonial Venezuelan cacao tradition with cutting-edge chocolate technology to create some of the world's most remarkable chocolates. El Rey now sells cacao nibs and cocoa powder, and has added three new formulations with higher cacao content to its popular Carenero Superior line.

**Chocovic S.A.**
*Barcelona Export Department:*
P.O. Box 34
08840 Viladecans (Barcelona), Spain
011 34 93 658 12 08 • 011 34 93 637 18 82 (fax)
*U.S. Distributor:*
**International Foods and Confections**
6590 Shiloh Road East, Suite C
Alpharetta, GA 30005
(770) 887-0201 • (770) 887-0086 (fax)
www.chocovic.es

This is another historic revival reminding us that the first chocolate factory of Europe was created in Barcelona. Chocovic, a modern reincarnation of the nineteenth-century Catalan Xocolat Arumi, is known for a wide range of chocolate products. Its real claim to chefs' attention in both Spain and the United States, however, has been launching three fine single-origin couvertures using beans from Grenada, Ecuador, and the Barlovento region of Venezuela. You might want to visit the company's cooking school, Aula Chocovic, where you are bound to meet some of the top pastry chefs of Catalunya.

**Guittard Chocolate Company**
10 Guittard Road
P.O. Box 4308
Burlingame, CA 94010
(800) 468-2462 • (650) 697-4427 • (650) 692-2761 (fax)
www. guittard.com • sales@guittard.com

A family-owned San Francisco chocolate manufacturer established by French-born Etienne Guittard in 1886, known as a maker of classic chocolate couvertures, confectionery coatings, Dutch-process cocoa powder, and other chocolate products. Cognoscenti also know that they produce fine boutique-style chocolates made from excellent-quality flavor beans, primarily Venezuelan *criollos* and *trinitarios* from small plantations. Guittard's Collection Etienne, a line launched in the spring of 2000, is now available to consumers through select specialty stores and mail-order sources.

## Omanhene Cocoa Bean Company

P.O. Box 22
Milwaukee, WI 53201-0022
(800) 588-2462 • (414) 332-6252 • (414) 332-5237 (fax)
www.omanhene.com

The brainchild of Steven Wallace, a former foreign exchange student to Ghana, this chocolate company is as Ghanaian as the Kente cloth pattern used on its wrapping. It is the only chocolate manufacturer in Ghana that exports to the United States. Omanhene produces only one chocolate, a dark milk chocolate with 48% cacao content and the clean flavor of the basic Ghana cacao, and a hot chocolate mix.

## Pâtisserie Chocolaterie Pralus S.A.

8 Rue Charles de Gaulle
42300 Roanne, France
011 33 4 77 71 24 10 • 011 33 4 77 70 30 63 (fax)
www.chocolat-pralus.com • praluschoc@aol.com

The Maison Pralus was founded in 1948 by Auguste Pralus, who won the coveted Meilleur Ouvrier de France award in 1955. The shop then became famous for the Praluline, a brioche flavored with pralines. Since 1988, under the guidance of Auguste's son François Pralus, the company is winning accolades for its roster of potent, finely textured chocolates made in small batches with beans from Madagascar (Pralus's favorite), Colombia, Java, Trinidad, and half a dozen other countries. All formulations sport a heaping 75% cacao content.

## Scharffen Berger Chocolate

914 Heinz Avenue
Berkeley, CA 94710
(510) 981-4050 • (510) 981-4051 (fax)
www.scharffen-berger.com

In 1996, champagne maker John Scharffenberger and physician Robert Steinberg joined forces to start up a small, one-of-a-kind chocolate factory that relies on time-tested artisanal methods and the best raw materials. The company's signature product is a flavorful dark couverture of high (70%) cacao content, made with a lavish blend of seven or eight flavor bean varieties from three continents. They have expanded to offer several new products including candy bars with crunchy cacao nibs, natural (nonalkalized) cocoa powder, and select roasted nibs. You will find these products in specialty stores such as Williams-Sonoma and Whole Foods, and at Scharffen Berger's retail store in Berkeley—the site of the company's new factory and café, where you can enjoy not only savory dishes but also desserts prepared with the company's chocolate.

## Valrhona

26600 Tain-L'Hermitage
France
011 33 475 75 07 90 90 • 011 33 475 75 08 05 17 (fax)
*U.S. Division:*
1901 Avenue of the Stars, Suite 1800
Los Angeles, CA 90067
(310) 277-0441 • (310) 277-7304 (fax)
www.valrhona.com

Synonymous with quality and finesse, this French manufacturer introduced the concept of *"grands crus"* to the world of modern chocolate. It was Valrhona that set chocolate lovers to talking of *goût de terroir* and the personality of different chocolates. They were also the first to make a selling point of the actual cacao percentage of the product.

### Jim Graham: Tessera Chocolate

742 Wesley Avenue
Evanston, IL 60202
(847) 491-1672
tessera@itsamac.com

Master chocolatier Jim Graham is known for his technical virtuosity and the exquisite hand-dipped chocolates he created during his long tenure at Mary Beth Liccioni's Chocolats le Français. Now he is the man professionals seek for special chocolate projects, courses, product development, and consulting.

### Peter Kump's New York Cooking School

50 West 23rd Street
New York, NY 10011
(212) 847-0700 • (212) 847-0719 (fax)
www.newyorkculinary.com

At this new incarnation of New York's beloved cooking school, you can take chocolate courses as part of the school's avocational program and attend chocolate demonstrations with renowned pastry chef and chocolate expert Nick Malgieri, the director of the pastry and baking program.

### Richardson Researchers, Inc.

23449 Foley Street
Hayward, CA 94545
(510) 785-1350 • (510) 785-6857 (fax)
www.richres.com

Combining lectures by chocolate technologist Terry Richardson, a respected teacher and consultant of the trade, and hands-on experiments at the facility's well-equipped laboratory, Richardson Researchers is the place to go for those serious professionals who want to know the nuts and bolts of chocolate manufacturing. The center offers week-long courses on Chocolate Technology, Gourmet Continental Chocolates, Confectionery Technology, and Compound Coating throughout the year.

## CANDY MAKERS, PASTRY SHOPS, AND BAKERIES

### Fran's Chocolates

1300 East Pike Street
Seattle, WA 98122-4020
(800) 422-FRAN • (206) 322-0233 • (206) 322-0452 (fax)
www.franschocolates.com

Fran Bigelow, one of America's premier chocolatiers, delivers intense flavor in a large range of candies and truffles made from first-rate chocolate. Look for Fran's two-ounce and mini candy bars with El Rey's Venezuelan cacao: Bucare with coffee beans or cacao nibs, and Caoba milk chocolate. Fran's two retail stores in Seattle are located near Bellevue Square and at University Village, not far from Husky Stadium. There you will find Fran's chocolate desserts and her addictive Nibbets—crunchy cacao nibs, the size of grape seeds, coated in Venezuelan chocolate.

### Jacques Torres Chocolates

66 Water Street
Brooklyn, NY 11201
(718) 875-9772 • (718) 875-2167 (fax)
www.mrchocolate.com

Celebrated pastry chef and master chocolatier Jacques Torres has crossed the East River to open a wholesale chocolate factory and retail shop in Brooklyn. While you sample Jacques's truffles made with natural ingredients and no preservatives or take a sip of coffee at the shop, you can see chocolate being made at the adjacent factory through a plate glass window.

### L. A. Burdick Chocolates

P.O. Box 63
52 Main Street
Walpole, NH 03608
(800) 229-2419 • (603) 756-4326 (fax)
www.burdickchocolate.com

Famed for his trademark chocolate mice (and most recently, whimsical penguins), Larry Burdick is also known for his uncompromising allegiance to the finest, freshest ingredients and exploratory vigor in expanding the palette of flavorings used in fine chocolate. For a taste of Larry's serious hot chocolate and Viennese pastries, visit Burdick's Cafés in Walpole, New Hampshire, and Cambridge, Massachusetts.

### La Brea Bakery

624 South La Brea
Los Angeles, CA 90036
(323) 939-6813
www.labreabakery.com

Bread and chocolate is a classic combination, but nobody does it better than pastry chef and baker Nancy Silverton—her chocolate cherry sourdough bread is legendary. You can find it at the retail shop of Nancy's La Brea Bakery. They will even ship it to you overnight.

### La Praline

Avenida Andres Bello Cruce con Tercera Transversal
Los Palos Grandes
Caracas, Venezuela
011 58 212 285 2475 • 011 58212 284 7986
011 58 212 285 9762 (fax)

At La Praline, Venezuela's most famous chocolate shop, Belgian-born Ludo and Lisette Gillis apply their Old World expertise to 100% Venezuelan chocolate. La Praline delivers edible art, from classic Belgian-style truffles with Venezuelan-grown macadamia nuts to fanciful sea creatures and erotic Indian temple scenes set in dark and white chocolate.

### Maison du Chocolat

225 Rue du Fauburg Saint-Honoré
75008 Paris, France
011 33 1 42 27 39 44 • 011 33 1 47 64 03 75 (fax)
*U.S. Location:*
1018 Madison Avenue
New York, NY 10021
(800) 988-5632 • (212) 744-7117
www.lamaisonduchocolat.com

Robert Linxe is a man who knows his beans. The founder of this exclusive Paris shop with branches in New York (Madison Avenue and Rockefeller Center) and other parts of the world is obsessed with the intrinsic flavor of the raw material as it comes from the world's cacao farms. His forte is matching each chocolate with the flavorings that will most perfectly bring out its uniqueness.

### Payard Patisserie & Bistro

1032 Lexington Avenue
New York, NY 10021
(212) 717-5252 • (212) 717-0986 (fax)
www.payard.com

François Payard, former pastry chef of Restaurant Daniel in Manhattan, now pours his prodigious energy into a range of creations from traditional *bûche de Noel* to original chocolate fantasies at his own bistro-cum-pastry shop. For a mouth-watering visual tour of Payard's offerings, visit the shop's on-line boutique.

### Rococo

321 Kings Road
London, United Kingdom SW3 5EP
011 44 20 7352 5857

Taste a geranium-scented artisan bar at Chantal Coady's charming Chelsea shop, and you'll understand why this is a haven for London's chocolate lovers.

Quelus, D. de. *Histoire naturelle du cacao, et du sucre: divisée en deux traités, qui contiennent plusiers faits nouveaux, & beaucoup d'observations egalement curieuses & utiles.* Paris: L. d'Houry, 1719.

Reyes, Humberto, et al. *Catálogo de cultivares del cacao criollo venezolano.* Venezuela: Fonaiap, n.d.

Ruz, Mario Humberto. *Un rostro encubierto: Los indios del Tabasco colonial.* Mexico: Instituto Nacional Indigenista, 1994.

Sahagún, Fray Bernardino de. *Historia general de las cosas de Nueva España.* Mexico: Editorial Porrúa, 1992.

Smith, Nigel J. H., et al. *Tropical Forests and Their Crops.* New York: Cornell University Press, 1992.

Szogyi, Alex, ed. *Chocolate: Food of the Gods.* Westport, CT: Greenwood Press, 1997.

Toxopeus, H., and G. Geisberger. "History of Cocoa and Cocoa Research in Indonesia." In *Archives of Cocoa Research* (1983).

Viso, Carlos. "En la almendra de cacao cabe el mundo." *Revista Bigott* 44 (1997–1998): 109–15.

Young, Allen M. *The Chocolate Tree: A Natural History of Cacao.* Washington, DC: Smithsonian Institution Press, 1994.

## CACAO JOURNALS, NEWSLETTERS, AND CHOCOLATE MAGAZINES

*Agrotropica.* Itabuna, Bahia: Centro de Pesquisas de Cacao (CEPEC).

*Annual Report on Cacao Research.* St. Augustine, Trinidad: Cocoa Research Unit.

*Archives of Cocoa Research.* Washington, DC: American Cocoa Research Institute.

*Chocolatier* (monthly magazine). New York, NY.

*Cocoa Research Unit Newsletter.* St. Augustine, Trinidad: Cocoa Research Unit.

*INGENIC (International Group for Genetic Improvement of Cocoa) Newsletter.*

*Tropical Agriculture.* St. Augustine, Trinidad: The University of the West Indies Press.

## CACAO RESEARCH INSTITUTES

ACRI  American Cocoa Research Institute

CATIE  Centro Agronómico Tropical de Investigaciones y Enseñanza (Turrialba, Costa Rica)

CEPLAC  Centro de Pesquisa do Cacao (Itabuna, Brazil)

CIRAD  Centre de Coopération Internationale en Récherche Agronomique pour le Développement (Montpellier, France)

CRIG  Cocoa Research Institute of Ghana

CRU  Cocoa Research Unit (St. Augustine, Trinidad)

ICG, T  International Cocoa Genebank of Trinidad

WACRI  West African Cocoa Research Institute

# Index

**A** "Age of Discovery" Vanilla-Scented Hot Chocolate, 173–74
Agostini, Philippe, 77, 114
*ahilados,* 50, 51
Aldea Toyo, 105
Alta Verapaz, 175
Amado, Jorge, 31
Amazon River basin, 10, 21, 33, 39, 58, 104, 106–8
*amelonado,* 34–35, 39, 84, 104, 105
Americans, preferences of, 119
Andean *criollos,* 68, 86, 93
*angoleta,* 84
aromas, 121–22
Aromatic Spice and Corn Blend for Hot Chocolate, 171
Arriba, 36, 39, 67, 70, 74, 85, 111, 123
Arzave, Angela, 158
Aztecs, 4, 12–17, 27, 129, 166, 173, 177

**B** Bacar Restaurant and Wine Salon, 158
Bahia, 31, 34–35, 39, 70, 73
bakeries, 188–89
bananas
    Chocolate-Coconut Soup with Fresh Bananas and Honey-Cocoa Wafers, 164–65
    Soft Chocolate Cake with Banana-Raisin Sauce and Lime Cream, 138–39
Baracoa, 78
Barcelona, 184
Barlovento, 7, 33, 34, 43, 50–51, 53, 55, 74, 77, 123
Barquisimeto, 62
Barry Callebaut, 78, 184
Bekele, Frances, 83, 112
Belize, 36
Bernachon, Maurice and Jean Jacques, 81
Bigelow, Fran, 136, 153, 188
black pod rot, 109
blended chocolate, 75–76, 79–81
bloom, 65, 120
Bolívar, Simón, 101
Borthomierth, Arsenio, 34, 51
Bouley Bakery, 138
Brachman, Wayne Harley, 142
Braker, Flo, 129, 146
Brazil, 34–35, 66, 70, 72, 85, 104
Bread Pudding, Caramelized Chocolate, with Coffee-Rum Sauce, 156–57
Brown, Joseph, 20
brownies

Honey-Cocoa Wafers (variation), 164–65
    Tropical Night Brownies, 128, 146
bulk beans, 72–73
Burdick, Larry, 144, 189

**C** cacao
    classifications of, 85
    cultivars of, 85–86, 88–95, 98–99, 101–2, 104–16
    cultivation of, 45–52
    diseases afflicting, 37–39
    fashion, 74–75
    fermenting and drying, 55–58, 66
    flavor beans vs. bulk beans, 67, 72–73
    future of, 41
    genome of, 39, 41, 83
    journals and newsletters, 192
    morphological types for, 83–84
    nibs and shells, 62
    origins of, 9–10
    polishing, 72
    quality testing, 60–61
    roasting, 62, 66
    trade, 59–60
    as tribute, 12, 13, 27
    worldwide migration of, 31–36
cacao balls
    Homemade Cacao Balls in the Style of the Paria Peninsula, 167–68
    Kekchi Cacao-Chile Balls, 175–76
    *sarrapia* and mamey sapote in, 179
    traditional handmade, 166
Cacao Barry, 184
    Equateur, 136
    Origine Rare, 78
Cacao Beans, Two-Toned Candied, Dipped in Chocolate, 130–31
cacao butter, 28, 63
cacao liquor, 28, 63
Cacao Nib Wafers and Rich Custard Ice Cream with Lavender-Vanilla Syrup, 150–52
Cadbury, 76
Cadbury, Richard, 28
cakes. *See also* tortes
    Scharffen Berger Roulade, 140–41
    Soft Chocolate Cake with Banana-Raisin Sauce and Lime Cream, 138–39
*calabacillo,* 84
Callebaut, 136, 138, 184
Cameroon, 34
Cañas, 3, 4
candy makers, 188–89

**H** Hacienda La Concepción, 7, 34, 50–51, 55, 57, 69
Haiti, 34, 72
Hermé, Pierre, 162
Hernández, 94
Herrera, Antonio de, 13, 86
Hershey, 76
Hévin, Jean-Paul, 132
Hibiscus Caramel, Creamy Chocolate Cheese Flan with, 154–55
Hispaniola, 72
Homemade Cacao Balls in the Style of the Paria Peninsula, 167–68
Honduras, 13
Honey-Cocoa Wafers, 164–65
hot chocolate
    "Age of Discovery" Vanilla-Scented Hot Chocolate, 173–74
    Aromatic Spice and Corn Blend for Hot Chocolate, 171
    from cacao balls, 170
    European adoption of, 17–20
    history of, 11, 13
    Spiced Hot Chocolate, 172
Hotel Sacher, 144

**I** Ibarra, 178
ice cream
    Cacao Nib Wafers and Rich Custard Ice Cream with Lavender-Vanilla Syrup, 150–52
    Chocolate Jasmine Ice Cream, 148–49
    Creamy Chocolate Cheese Flan with Hibiscus Caramel (variation), 154–55
Imperial College of Tropical Agriculture, 25, 37–38, 108, 112
Imperial College Selections (ICS), 108, 113–15
Indonesia, 31, 35, 37, 66, 72, 78
International Cocoa Genebank of Trinidad (ICG, T), 41, 108, 109, 113
Iquitos Marañón River, 108
Iquitos Mixed Calabacillo (IMC), 106, 108, 110, 116
Ivory Coast, 34, 71, 72, 73

**J** Japanese, preferences of, 119, 122
Jasmine Ice Cream, Chocolate, 148–49
Jauco River, 1, 3, 5
Java, 31, 35, 37, 66, 67, 71, 74, 76
journals, 192

**K** Kekchi Cacao-Chile Balls, 175–76
Kekchi Maya, 175
Kump, Peter, 187

**L** labeling, 31, 79–80
La Brea Bakery, 189
Lachanaud, Philip, 85
La Guaira, 27
Lake Maracaibo, 10, 15, 27, 48, 74, 86, 88
La Locomotora, 28
La Molina, 93
La Pagerie, 104
La Praline, 189
La Reunion, 59
La Sabaneta, 69, 98
Lavender-Vanilla Syrup, Cacao Nib Wafers and Rich Custard Ice Cream with, 150–52
Liccioni, Mary Beth, 187
Lindt, Rodolphe, 29, 64
Lindt Excellence, 138
Linnaeus, Carolus, 7, 9
Linxe, Robert, 189
Los Angeles, 189

Madagascar, 71, 74, 123
**M** magazines, 192
Magdalena, 74
mail order, 186
Maison du Chocolat, 189
Malaysia, 31, 35, 57, 71, 72, 120
Malgieri, Nick, 187
malt, 122
mamey sapote, 88, 167, 179
Mango, Pecan–Guaranda Chocolate Tart with Papaya and, 142–43
Maracaibo. *See* Lake Maracaibo
Martinique, 104
Marper Farm, 38, 108
Matos, Desideria, 3
Mavaca River, 58
Maya, 11, 36, 129, 160, 166, 173, 175
Maya-Mediterranean Chocolate Rice Pudding, 160–61
McGee, Harold, 129, 132
*medianería,* 51
mélangeur, 28
Merian, Maria Sibylla, 40
Mérida, Venezuela, 4, 90, 92
Mérida, Yucatán, 160
*metates,* 18, 29, 166
Mexía de Liendo, Doña Catalina, 101
Mexico, 10, 11, 13, 14, 16, 24, 74. *See also individual locations*
milk chocolate
    added ingredients in, 63–64, 122

origins of, 31
    tempering, 134–35
Mixtecs, 14
Moctezuma, 14
moles, 18, 177
Mole Xalapeño, 177–79
moniliasis, 89

*Nacional,* 35, 36
Nanay, 108, 109
Nestlé, 76
newsletters, 192
New York, 130, 138, 142, 187, 189
Nicaragua, 13, 24, 36
Nigeria, 34, 71, 73

Oaxaca, 13, 14, 188
Ocumare, 68, 95, 102, 116
Olmecs, 11
Omanhene chocolate, 80, 158, 185
Omanhene Chocolate–Coconut Crème Stack, 158–59
Orinoco River basin, 24, 25, 26, 58

*pajarito,* 93
Papantla, 4, 174
Papaya, Pecan–Guaranda Chocolate Tart with Mango and, 142–43
Papua New Guinea, 71, 123, 175
Paria Peninsula, 34, 69, 74, 146, 166, 167
Parinari, 108
Paris, 189
pastry shops, 188–89
Pâtisserie Chocolaterie Pralus, 185
Payard, François, 189
Pecan–Guaranda Chocolate Tart with Mango and Papaya, 142–43
Pérez, Estela, 177
Peru, 38, 106, 108, 110, 111, 116
Peter, Daniel, 31
Pfeiffer, Jacquy, 187
Philippines, 31, 35, 37
*pinole,* 171
Pistachio, Coconut, and Pearl Tapioca Sauce, Chocolate Croquettes with, 162–63
Plan Cacao, 117
plantations, 21–22, 45–46, 50–51
Pointe-á-Pitre, 166
pollination, 109
*porcelana,* 15, 45, 48, 86, 88–90
Pound, F. J., 38, 39, 106, 111, 113, 116
Pralus, Auguste, 185

Pralus, François, 162, 185
preferences, 119
Princess Pudding, 153
puddings
    Caramelized Chocolate Bread Pudding with Coffee-Rum Sauce, 156–57
    Maya-Mediterranean Chocolate Rice Pudding, 160–61
    Princess Pudding, 153
Puebla City, 177
Pueblo Viejo, 111
Puerto Cabello, 74, 123

raisins
    Caramelized Chocolate Bread Pudding with Coffee-Rum Sauce, 156–57
    Soft Chocolate Cake with Banana-Raisin Sauce and Lime Cream, 138–39
Redi, Francesco, 149
*refractarios,* 39
Reneau, Julie, 109
research institutes, 37, 41, 192
Reyes, Humberto, 25
Reyes, Lilian, 116
Reyes, Silvino, 51
Rice Pudding, Maya-Mediterranean Chocolate, 160–61
Richardson, Terry, 134, 135, 188
Río Caribe, 69, 74, 116, 167
Rio Negro, 107
Rococo, 189
Rodríguez, Ana, 166, 167, 170
Rosenberg, Kai, 98
Roulade, Scharffen Berger, 140–41
royal cacao, 36

Sachertorte, Classic, 144–45
Sahagún, Bernardino de, 14, 15, 16
salt, 122
Sánchez, 72, 73
San Francisco, 79, 140, 158, 184, 187
San Juan de Lagunillas, 45, 90, 91
San Juan Estate, 70, 77, 78, 114
San Pedro Sula, 105
Santa Clara de Choroní, 98
Santa Maria, Domingo de, 14
Scavinas, 110, 111
Scavino, Eduardo, 111
Scharffenberger, John, 81, 185
Scharffen Berger chocolate, 81, 123, 132, 140, 154, 185
Scharffen Berger Roulade, 140–41
Schlageter Jorge Redmond, 184
Seasons of My Heart Cooking School, 188

Seattle, 136, 188
Sierra de Perijá, 90
Silverton, Nancy, 189
Soconosco, 12, 13, 27
Soft Chocolate Cake with Banana-Raisin Sauce and Lime
    Cream, 138–39
Soup, Chocolate-Coconut, with Fresh Bananas and
    Honey-Cocoa Wafers, 164–65
Spain, 17, 32, 171, 173
Spiced Hot Chocolate, 172
Steinberg, Robert, 81, 185
Sukha, Darin, 61, 109
Sulawesi, 71, 72
Sur del Lago, 68, 86, 88, 90, 93
Surinam, 85
Swiss, preferences of, 119, 126

*T* Tabasco, 13, 58, 70, 104
tarts
    Pecan–Guaranda Chocolate Tart with Mango and
        Papaya, 142–43
    Princess Pudding (variation), 153
    shell, 142
tasting, 120–24, 126
tea
    Earl Grey Whipped Cream, 140–41
    Scharffen Berger Roulade, 140–41
tempering, 134–35
Tenochtitlán, 12, 13
texture, 126
*Theobroma bicolor,* 9, 11
*Theobroma cacao,* 7, 9, 15
*Theobroma grandiflora,* 9
*Theobroma leiocarpa,* 22
*Theobroma patashte,* 9
*Theobroma pentagona,* 84, 94
*Theobroma speciosum,* 10
Tía Locha, 90
Tlachinollan, 176
Torres, Jacques, 188
Torres, Raquel, 177
tortes
    Classic Sachertorte, 144–45
    Deep Chocolate Torte, 136
Totomixtlahuacan, 176
Tourondel, Laurent, 129, 130, 150
tours, 187–88
Trilling, Susana, 188
Trincheras, 68
Trinidad, 24–25, 34, 36, 41, 51, 59, 60, 67, 70, 72, 78,
    108, 112, 114

Trinidad Select Hybrids (TSH), 39, 116
*trinitarios,* 112–16
    color of, 120
    *criollos* and *forasteros* vs., 26
    grades of, 67
    Imperial College Selections (ICS), 113–15
    Ocumare and IMC 67, 68, 116
    origins of, 24–25
    TSH, 39, 116
Tropical–Night Brownies, 128, 146
Truffles, Chocolate-Cheese, 132–33
Two-Toned Candied Cacao Beans Dipped in Chocolate,
    130–31

*U* Ucayali River, 111

*V* Valrhona, 185
    Chocolate Noir de Domaine Gran Couva, 77, 78
    Guanaja, 130
    Jivara, 148
    Manjari, 120, 124, 138, 162
    Pur Caraïbe, 138, 160, 172
Van Houten, Conrad, 28, 34
vanilla, 122, 173, 174
Vanilla-Scented Whipped Cream, 144–45
Venezuela, 24, 33, 34, 36, 52, 59, 68–69, 74, 85, 86–102,
    116, 117, 184, 189. *See also individual locations*
Vergara y Vergara, José Maria, 16

*w* wafers
    Cacao Nib Wafers, 150–52
    Honey-Cocoa Wafers, 164–65
Wallace, Steven, 185
Warneau, Luiz Frederico, 34
West Africa, 21, 31, 35, 66, 72, 104, 119, 122, 123
whipped cream
    Earl Grey Whipped Cream, 140–41
    *Theobroma bicolor* as, 11
    Vanilla-Scented Whipped Cream, 144–45
Wilbur Chocolate Company, 74
witches' broom, 38, 39, 106, 108, 110

*X* Xalapa, 28, 177
Xico, 177
Xocolat Arumi, 30, 77, 184
Xoconochco, 12, 13

*y* Yaguaraparo, 69, 166, 167
Yanomami, 58
Yosses, Bill, 138
Yucatán, 36, 160